Exodus Story

Exodus Story

by

Daniel A. Elias

Tzeruf Co

Author: *Daniel A. Elias, J.D.*

Publisher: Tzeruf Co
235 S Lyon Ave # 39
Hemet, CA 92543 USA
mail@tzeruf.com

SAN Number 853-0203

© 2013 by Tzeruf Co.
Printed in USA

All rights reserved. No part of this publication may be reproduced or transmitted in any form or by any means, electronic or mechanical, including photocopying, recording, or by any information storage an d retrieval system, without permission in writing from Tzeruf Co.

First Edition Published 2013

Publisher's Cataloging-in-Publication data

Elias, Daniel A..

Exodus Story
p. cm.

English Paperback   ISBN   978-0-9792826-4-5

1. Religion 2. Bible. 3. Hebrew

This book is dedicated to

Moses, and

all the Tzadikim of this generation,

and to all the Tzadikim who are at rest in the dust.

Table of Contents

Table of Contents VII

Preface IX

Seder Laws 11

Parashat Shemot 23

    Chapter 1 23

    Chapter 2 27

    Chapter 3 32

    Chapter 4 37

    Chapter 5 43

    Chapter 6 48

Parashat - Vaera 49

    Chapter 6 cont 49

    Chapter 7 54

    Chapter 8 60

    Chapter 9 67

PARASHAT 3 - BO 75

    CHAPTER 10 75

    CHAPTER 11 82

    CHAPTER 12 84

    CHAPTER 13 95

PARASHAT 4 - BESHALACH 99

    CHAPTER 13 CONT 99

    CHAPTER 14 100

    CHAPTER 15 107

Preface

Translations. The objective of the translated Hebrew in this book is;
  1) to help one to be fluent in the reading of Hebrew,
  2) to learn Hebrew vocabulary by seeing directly below the Hebrew word what the English translation is.
  3) to memorize parts of the verses of the sacred scriptures
  4) to easily increase kavanah or thought intension when praying the Psalms.
  5) to feed the soul the effects of bible code while reading the biblical verses

One translated Hebrew word of a verse contains so much subtle information. There is the root, the prefix, the affix, dropped weak letters, gutturals, dagesh lene, dagesh forte, it's sentence grammatical name, etc. Much of the english grammar has been left out by necessity; ie. the translation "the" was put in only when there was a specific prefix letter Heh, not where a prefix has a patach.

Every expression in the [ongoing] present tense can variably be expressed in the future tense as well as in the past tense because anything that is ongoing in the present tense has already happened and will continue to happen.

I would have preferred to translate the tenses of the verbs as they actually appear instead of looking to the sentence meaning to infer the past, present or future. This best reflects the base thought of Hebrew language. However in order to make the text as simple to understand for the majority of people who do not understand this concept I have put in the inferred verb tenses.

Seder Laws

Pesach commemorates the day the Children of Israel reached the Red Sea and witnessed both the miraculous "Splitting of the Sea," the drowning of all the Egyptian chariots, horses and soldiers that pursued them, and the Passage of the Red Sea. According to the Midrash, only Pharaoh was spared to give testimony to the miracle that occurred.

In the first month, on the fourteenth day of the month between the two evenings is the LORD'S Passover. And on the fifteenth day of the same month is the feast of unleavened bread unto the LORD; seven days ye shall eat unleavened bread. In the first day ye shall have a holy convocation; ye shall do no manner of servile work. And ye shall bring an offering made by fire unto the LORD seven days; in the seventh day is a holy convocation; ye shall do no manner of servile work.

Called Hag HaMatzot (festival of the Matza) in the Torah, the commandment to keep Passover is recorded in the Book of Leviticus.

Leviticus 23:5

בַּחֹדֶשׁ הָרִאשׁוֹן בְּאַרְבָּעָה עָשָׂר לַחֹדֶשׁ
to month   - fourteenth -   the first   in month

בֵּין הָעַרְבַּיִם פֶּסַח לַיהוָה׃
to ihvh   pesach   the evenings   between

5 In the fourteenth day of the first month at even is the LORD'S passover.

וּבַחֲמִשָּׁה עָשָׂר יוֹם לַחֹדֶשׁ הַזֶּה
the this   to month   day   - fifteenth -   -and

חַג הַמַּצּוֹת לַיהוָה
to ihvh   the unleavened bread   feast

$$\text{שִׁבְעַת יָמִים מַצּוֹת תֹּאכֵלוּ׃}$$

seven   days   unleavened   you eat it

6 And on the fifteenth day of the same month is the feast of unleavened bread unto the LORD: seven days ye must eat unleavened bread.

$$\text{בַּיּוֹם הָרִאשׁוֹן מִקְרָא־קֹדֶשׁ יִהְיֶה לָכֶם}$$

in day   the first   holy - meeting   ihvh   to you

$$\text{כָּל־מְלֶאכֶת עֲבֹדָה לֹא תַעֲשׂוּ׃}$$

work - all   service   not   you do it

7 In the first day ye shall have an holy convocation: ye shall do no servile work therein.

$$\text{וְהִקְרַבְתֶּם אִשֶּׁה לַיהוָה שִׁבְעַת יָמִים}$$

and cause you to offering   fire   to ihvh   seven   days

$$\text{בַּיּוֹם הַשְּׁבִיעִי מִקְרָא־קֹדֶשׁ}$$

in day   the seventh   holy - meeting

$$\text{כָּל־מְלֶאכֶת עֲבֹדָה לֹא תַעֲשׂוּ׃}$$

work - all   service   not   you do it

8 But ye shall offer an offering made by fire unto the LORD seven days: in the seventh day is an holy convocation: ye shall do no servile work therein.

REMEMBER

The Biblical commandments concerning the Passover (and the Feast of Unleavened Bread) stress the importance of remembering:

DEUTERONOMY 16:12

And thou shalt remember that thou wast a bondman in Egypt; and thou shalt observe and do these statutes."

EXODUS 13:3

Remember this day, in which you came out of Egypt, out of the house of bondage, for by strength the hand of the LORD brought you out from this place.

A Memorial

Exodus 12:14

וְהָיָה הַיּוֹם הַזֶּה לָכֶם לְזִכָּרוֹן

to remembrance   to you   the this   the day and it be

וְחַגֹּתֶם אֹתוֹ חַג לַיהוָה לְדֹרֹתֵיכֶם חֻקַּת עוֹלָם תְּחָגֻּהוּ׃

you feast it   forever   statute   to your generations   to ihvh   festival   to it   and festival

12:14 And this day shall be unto you for a memorial; and ye shall keep it a feast to the LORD throughout your generations; ye shall keep it a feast by an ordinance for ever.

Remove Chametz

To remove all chametz from one's home, including things made with chametz, before the first day of Passover.

Exodus 12:15

שִׁבְעַת יָמִים מַצּוֹת תֹּאכֵלוּ

you eat   unleavened bread   days   seven

אַךְ בַּיּוֹם הָרִאשׁוֹן תַּשְׁבִּיתוּ שְּׂאֹר מִבָּתֵּיכֶם

from your house   remain   you put away   the first   in day   certainly

כִּי כָּל־אֹכֵל חָמֵץ וְנִכְרְתָה הַנֶּפֶשׁ הַהִוא מִיִּשְׂרָאֵל

from Israel   the it   the soul   and cut off   yeast   eat – all   like

מִיּוֹם הָרִאשֹׁן עַד־יוֹם הַשְּׁבִעִי׃

the seventh   day – till   the first   from day

15 Seven days shall ye eat unleavened bread; even the first day ye shall put away leaven out of your houses: for whosoever eateth leavened bread from the first day until the seventh day, that soul shall be cut off from Israel.

Disposing of Leaven

The biblical regulations for the observance of the festival require that all leavening be disposed of before the beginning of the 15th of Nisan.

Eating Unleavened Bread

Exodus 13:6

שִׁבְעַת יָמִים תֹּאכַל מַצֹּת

seven　　days　　you eater　　unleavened

וּבַיּוֹם הַשְּׁבִיעִי חַג לַיהוָה׃

and in day　　the seventh　　holiday　　to ihvh

6 Seven days thou shalt eat unleavened bread, and in the seventh day shall be a feast to the LORD.

Unleavened Bread with Bitter herbs

with unleavened bread and bitter herbs.

Exodus 12:8

וְאָכְלוּ אֶת־הַבָּשָׂר בַּלַּיְלָה הַזֶּה צְלִי־אֵשׁ

and they eat　　the flesh – that　　in night　　the this　　fire – roast

וּמַצּוֹת עַל־מְרֹרִים יֹאכְלֻהוּ׃

and unleavened bread　　bitter herbs – upon　　they eat it

8 And they shall eat the flesh in that night, roast with fire, and unleavened bread; and with bitter herbs they shall eat it.

Seven Days Unleavened Bread

Exodus 23:18

בָּרִאשֹׁן בְּאַרְבָּעָה עָשָׂר יוֹם לַחֹדֶשׁ בָּעֶרֶב

in first　　- in fourteenth -　　day　　to month　　in evening

תֹּאכְלוּ מַצֹּת עַד יוֹם הָאֶחָד וְעֶשְׂרִים לַחֹדֶשׁ בָּעֶרֶב׃

you will eat　　unleavened bread　　till　　day　　the first　　and twentieth　　to month　　in evening

18 In the first month, on the fourteenth day of the month at even, ye shall eat unleavened bread, until the one and twentieth day of the month at even.

שִׁבְעַת יָמִים שְׂאֹר לֹא יִמָּצֵא בְּבָתֵּיכֶם

seven　　days　　remains　　not　　it found　　in your houses

כִּי כָּל־אֹכֵל מַחְמֶצֶת
leaven   eater – all   like

וְנִכְרְתָה הַנֶּפֶשׁ הַהִוא מֵעֲדַת יִשְׂרָאֵל
Israel   from congregation   the it   the soul   and cut off

בַּגֵּר וּבְאֶזְרַח הָאָרֶץ׃
the land   and in born   in stranger

19 Seven days shall there be no leaven found in your houses: for whosoever eateth that which is leavened, even that soul shall be cut off from the congregation of Israel, whether he be a stranger, or born in the land.

כָּל־מַחְמֶצֶת לֹא תֹאכֵלוּ בְּכֹל מוֹשְׁבֹתֵיכֶם תֹּאכְלוּ מַצּוֹת׃
unleavened   you eat it   your habitations   in all   you eat it   not   from leaven – all

20 Ye shall eat nothing leavened; in all your habitations shall ye eat unleavened bread.

Unblemished Lamb

An unblemished lamb or goat is to be set apart on Nisan 10. Four days before the Exodus, the Hebrews were commanded to set aside a lamb and inspect it daily for blemishes.

Exodus 12:3

דַּבְּרוּ אֶל־כָּל־עֲדַת יִשְׂרָאֵל לֵאמֹר
to say   Israel   congregation - all – unto   you speak

בֶּעָשֹׂר לַחֹדֶשׁ הַזֶּה
the this   to month   in tenth

וְיִקְחוּ לָהֶם אִישׁ שֶׂה לְבֵית־אָבֹת שֶׂה לַבָּיִת׃
to house   lamb   fathers – to house   lamb   man   to them   and they take

3 Speak ye unto all the congregation of Israel, saying, In the tenth day of this month they shall take to them every man a lamb, according to the house of their fathers, a lamb for an house:

No Bones Broken

One had to be careful not to break any bones from the offering,

Exodus 12:46

בְּבַיִת אֶחָד יֵאָכֵל

he eats   one   in house

לֹא־תוֹצִיא מִן־הַבַּיִת מִן־הַבָּשָׂר חוּצָה

outside   the flesh – from   the house – from   you go out – not

וְעֶצֶם לֹא תִשְׁבְּרוּ־בוֹ:

in it – you break it   not   and exactly

46 In one house shall it be eaten; thou shalt not carry forth ought of the flesh abroad out of the house; neither shall ye break a bone thereof.

Specific Place

The sacrifices may only be performed in a specific place prescribed by God (for Judaism, Jerusalem and for Samaritans Mount Grezim).

When to Slaughter & Eat

and slaughtered on Nisan 14 "between the two evenings"

and eat it that night, which was the 15th of Nisan.

Exodus 12:6

וְהָיָה לָכֶם לְמִשְׁמֶרֶת עַד אַרְבָּעָה עָשָׂר יוֹם לַחֹדֶשׁ הַזֶּה

the this   to month   day   ten   four   till   to keep it up   to them   and it be

וְשָׁחֲטוּ אֹתוֹ כֹּל קְהַל עֲדַת־יִשְׂרָאֵל בֵּין הָעַרְבָּיִם:

the evening   between   Israel – congregation   assembly   all   to it   and you butcher it

6 And ye shall keep it up until the fourteenth day of the same month: and the whole assembly of the congregation of Israel shall kill it in the evening.

Roast Method

Roasted, without the removal of its internal organs and had to be roasted, without its head, feet, or inner organs being removed

Exodus 12:9

אַל־תֹּאכְלוּ מִמֶּנּוּ נָא וּבָשֵׁל מְבֻשָּׁל בַּמָּיִם
in water   soaked   and raw   now   from it   you eat – don't

כִּי אִם־צְלִי־אֵשׁ רֹאשׁוֹ עַל־כְּרָעָיו וְעַל־קִרְבּוֹ׃
his insides - and upon   his legs - upon   his head   fire – roast – if   like

9 Eat not of it raw, nor sodden at all with water, but roast with fire; his head with his legs, and with the purtenance thereof.

Loins Girded

The biblical regulations pertaining to the original Passover also included how the meal is to be eaten:

Exodus 12:11

וְכָכָה תֹּאכְלוּ אֹתוֹ מָתְנֵיכֶם חֲגֻרִים
girded   from your loins   to it   you eat it   and thus

נַעֲלֵיכֶם בְּרַגְלֵיכֶם וּמַקֶּלְכֶם בְּיֶדְכֶם
in your hand   and your staff   your feet   your shoes

וַאֲכַלְתֶּם אֹתוֹ בְּחִפָּזוֹן פֶּסַח הוּא לַיהוָה׃
to ihvh   it   passover   in haste   to it   and your eat

11 And thus shall ye eat it; with your loins girded, your shoes on your feet, and your staff in your hand; and ye shall eat it in haste: it is the LORD'S passover.

Pesach

The verb "pasàch" (Hebrew: פָּסַח) is first mentioned in the Torah account of the Exodus from Egypt

Exodus 12:23

וְעָבַר יְהוָה לִנְגֹּף אֶת־מִצְרַיִם
Egyptians – that   to strike   ihvh   and will pass

וְרָאָה אֶת־הַדָּם עַל־הַמַּשְׁקוֹף וְעַל שְׁתֵּי הַמְּזוּזֹת
the door posts   two   and upon   lintel – upon   the blood – that   and see

וּפָסַח יְהוָה עַל־הַפֶּתַח
the opening – upon   ihvh   and will pass over

וְלֹא יִתֵּן הַמַּשְׁחִית לָבֹא אֶל־בָּתֵּיכֶם לִנְגֹּף׃
to strike   your houses – unto   to come   the destroyer   he will give   and not

23 For the LORD will pass through to smite the Egyptians; and when he seeth the blood upon the lintel, and on the two side posts, the LORD will pass over the door, and will not suffer the destroyer to come in unto your houses to smite you.

During the day on the 14th of Nisan, they were to slaughter the animal and use its blood to mark their lintels and door posts. Up until midnight on the 15th of Nisan, they were to consume the lamb. Each family (or group of families) gathered together to eat a meal that included the meat of the Korban Pesach while the Tenth Plague ravaged Egypt.

When the Temple in Jerusalem was standing, the focus of the Passover festival was the Korban Pesach (lit. "Pesach sacrifice," also known as the "Paschal Lamb"). Every family large enough to completely consume a young lamb or wild goat was required to offer one for sacrifice at the Jewish Temple on the afternoon of the 14th day of Nisan,

If the family was too small to finish eating the entire offering in one sitting, an offering was made for a group of families. The sacrifice could not be offered with anything leavened.

Leftovers Burned

Nothing of the sacrifice on which the sun rises may be eaten, but must be burned. and none of the meat could be left over by morning.

Exodus 12:10

וְלֹא־תוֹתִירוּ מִמֶּנּוּ עַד־בֹּקֶר

morning – till   from you   it remain - and not

וְהַנֹּתָר מִמֶּנּוּ עַד־בֹּקֶר בָּאֵשׁ תִּשְׂרֹפוּ׃

you burn it   in fire   morning – till   from it   and the remainder

10 And ye shall let nothing of it remain until the morning; and that which remaineth of it until the morning ye shall burn with fire.

Seventh day a holiday

On this final day of Passover we strive for the highest level of freedom, and focus on the Final Redemption.

Following the Baal Shem Tov's custom, we end Passover with "Moshiach's Feast"—a festive meal complete with matzah and four cups of wine, during which we celebrate the imminent arrival of the Messiah. The feast begins before sunset and continues until after nightfall.

Exodus 13:6

שִׁבְעַת יָמִים תֹּאכַל מַצֹּת וּבַיּוֹם הַשְּׁבִיעִי חַג לַיהוָה׃

to ihvh   festival   the seventh   and in day   unleavened   you will eat   days   seven

6 Seven days thou shalt eat unleavened bread, and in the seventh day shall be a feast to the LORD.

LEVITICUS 23:8

בַּיּוֹם הַשְּׁבִיעִי מִקְרָא־קֹדֶשׁ
holy - meeting   the seventh in day

כָּל־מְלֶאכֶת עֲבֹדָה לֹא תַעֲשׂוּ׃
you will do not service   work - all

8 ....in the seventh day is an holy convocation: ye shall do no servile work therein.

Together with Shavuot ("Pentecost") and Sukkot ("Tabernacles"), Passover is one of the three pilgrimage festivals (Shalosh Regalim) during which the entire Jewish populace historically made a pilgrimage to the Temple in Jerusalem.

Counting the Omer

וּסְפַרְתֶּם לָכֶם מִמָּחֳרַת הַשַּׁבָּת
the shabbat   from morrow   to you   and you count

מִיּוֹם הֲבִיאֲכֶם אֶת־עֹמֶר הַתְּנוּפָה
the wave offering   omar - that   you brought   from day

שֶׁבַע שַׁבָּתוֹת תְּמִימֹת תִּהְיֶינָה׃
it will be   complete   sabbaths   seven

15 And ye shall count unto you from the morrow after the sabbath, from the day that ye brought the sheaf of the wave offering; seven sabbaths shall be complete:

עַד מִמָּחֳרַת הַשַּׁבָּת הַשְּׁבִיעִת
the seventh   the sabbath   from after   till

תִּסְפְּרוּ חֲמִשִּׁים יוֹם
day   fifty   you number it

וְהִקְרַבְתֶּם מִנְחָה חֲדָשָׁה לַיהוָה׃
to ihvh   holy   offering   and you cause meat offer

16 Even unto the morrow after the seventh sabbath shall ye number fifty days; and ye shall offer a new meat offering unto the LORD.

Parashat Shemot

Chapter 1

[פרשת שמות]
ספר שמות פרק א

וְאֵ֗לֶּה שְׁמוֹת֙ בְּנֵ֣י יִשְׂרָאֵ֔ל
Israel · sons · names · now these

הַבָּאִ֖ים מִצְרָ֑יְמָה אֵ֣ת יַעֲקֹ֔ב אִ֥ישׁ וּבֵית֖וֹ בָּֽאוּ׃
they came · and his house · man · Jacob · that · towards Egypt · the coming ones

1 Now these are the names of the children of Israel, which came into Egypt; every man and his household came with Jacob.

רְאוּבֵ֣ן שִׁמְע֔וֹן לֵוִ֖י וִיהוּדָֽה׃
and Judah · Levi · Simeon · Reuben

2 Reuben, Simeon, Levi, and Judah,

יִשָּׂשכָ֥ר זְבוּלֻ֖ן וּבִנְיָמִֽן׃
and Benjamin · Zebulun · Isschacar

3 Issachar, Zebulun, and Benjamin,

דָּ֥ן וְנַפְתָּלִ֖י גָּ֥ד וְאָשֵֽׁר׃
and Asher · Gad · and Naphtali · Dan

4 Dan, and Naphtali, Gad, and Asher.

וַֽיְהִ֗י כָּל־נֶ֛פֶשׁ יֹצְאֵ֥י יֶֽרֶךְ־יַעֲקֹ֖ב שִׁבְעִ֣ים נָ֑פֶשׁ
soul · seventy · Jacob-descended · coming out ones · soul-all · and it was

וְיוֹסֵ֖ף הָיָ֥ה בְמִצְרָֽיִם׃
in Egypt · was · Joseph

5 And all the souls that came out of the loins of Jacob were seventy souls: for Joseph was in Egypt already.

וַיָּ֤מָת יוֹסֵף֙ וְכָל־אֶחָ֔יו
his brothers-and all · Joseph · and he died

וְכֹ֖ל הַדּ֥וֹר הַהֽוּא׃
the it · the generation · and all

6 And Joseph died, and all his brethren, and all that generation.

וּבְנֵ֣י יִשְׂרָאֵ֗ל פָּר֧וּ וַֽיִּשְׁרְצ֛וּ
and they roaming · they fruitful · Israel · and sons

וַיִּרְבּ֥וּ וַיַּֽעַצְמ֖וּ בִּמְאֹ֣ד מְאֹ֑ד
greatly · in greatly · and they grew · and they increased

וַתִּמָּלֵ֥א הָאָ֖רֶץ אֹתָֽם׃
with them   the land   and it was filled

7 And the children of Israel were fruitful, and increased abundantly, and multiplied, and waxed exceeding mighty; and the land was filled with them.

פ

וַיָּ֥קָם מֶֽלֶךְ־חָדָ֖שׁ עַל־מִצְרָ֑יִם אֲשֶׁ֥ר לֹֽא־יָדַ֖ע אֶת־יוֹסֵֽף׃
Joseph – that   he knew - not   which   Egypt - upon   new - king   and he arose

8 Now there arose up a new king over Egypt, which knew not Joseph.

וַיֹּ֖אמֶר אֶל־עַמּ֑וֹ
his people - unto   and he said

הִנֵּ֗ה עַ֚ם בְּנֵ֣י יִשְׂרָאֵ֔ל רַ֥ב וְעָצ֖וּם מִמֶּֽנּוּ׃
than us   and powerful   many   Israel   sons   people   here

9 And he said unto his people, Behold, the people of the children of Israel are more and mightier than we:

הָ֥בָה נִֽתְחַכְּמָ֖ה ל֑וֹ פֶּן־יִרְבֶּ֗ה
he increase - lest   to him   we it deal wisely   the ready

וְהָיָ֞ה כִּֽי־תִקְרֶ֤אנָה מִלְחָמָה֙ וְנוֹסַ֤ף גַּם־הוּא֙ עַל־שֹׂ֣נְאֵ֔ינוּ
haters of us - upon   he - also   and join   war   it proclaim - like   and it be

וְנִלְחַם־בָּ֖נוּ וְעָלָ֥ה מִן־הָאָֽרֶץ׃
the land - from   and ascend   in us - and they war

10 Come on, let us deal wisely with them; lest they multiply, and it come to pass, that, when there falleth out any war, they join also unto our enemies, and fight against us, and so get them up out of the land.

וַיָּשִׂ֤ימוּ עָלָיו֙ שָׂרֵ֣י מִסִּ֔ים לְמַ֥עַן עַנֹּת֖וֹ בְּסִבְלֹתָ֑ם
in burdening them   his affliction   to end   tribute   officers   upon him   and they put

וַיִּ֜בֶן עָרֵ֤י מִסְכְּנוֹת֙ לְפַרְעֹ֔ה אֶת־פִּתֹ֖ם וְאֶת־רַעַמְסֵֽס׃
Raamses - and that   Pithom - that   to Pharaoh   provisions   cities   and he built

11 Therefore they did set over them taskmasters to afflict them with their burdens. And they built for Pharaoh treasure cities, Pithom and Raamses.

וְכַאֲשֶׁר֙ יְעַנּ֣וּ אֹת֔וֹ כֵּ֥ן יִרְבֶּ֖ה וְכֵ֣ן יִפְרֹ֑ץ
he breaking forth   and thus   he multiplied   thus   to him   they afflicted   and when

וַיָּקֻ֕צוּ מִפְּנֵ֖י בְּנֵ֥י יִשְׂרָאֵֽל׃
Israel   sons   from face   and they irritated

12 But the more they afflicted them, the more they multiplied and grew. And they were grieved because of the children of Israel.

וַיַּעֲבִ֧דוּ מִצְרַ֛יִם אֶת־בְּנֵ֥י יִשְׂרָאֵ֖ל בְּפָֽרֶךְ׃
in rigour   Israel   sons – that   Egyptians   and they served

13 And the Egyptians made the children of Israel to serve with rigour:

וַיְמָרְרוּ אֶת־חַיֵּיהֶם בַּעֲבֹדָה קָשָׁה בְּחֹמֶר וּבִלְבֵנִים
and they made bitter their lives - that in service hard in mortar and in bricks

וּבְכָל־עֲבֹדָה בַּשָּׂדֶה
service - and in all in field

אֵת כָּל־עֲבֹדָתָם אֲשֶׁר־עָבְדוּ בָהֶם בְּפָרֶךְ:
that all their service which - they served in them in rigour

14 And they made their lives bitter with hard bondage, in mortar, and in brick, and in all manner of service in the field: all their service, wherein they made them serve, was with rigour.

וַיֹּאמֶר מֶלֶךְ מִצְרַיִם לַמְיַלְּדֹת הָעִבְרִיֹּת
and he said king Egypt to midwives the Hebrew women

אֲשֶׁר שֵׁם הָאַחַת שִׁפְרָה וְשֵׁם הַשֵּׁנִית פּוּעָה:
which name the one Shiphrah and name the second Puah

15 And the king of Egypt spake to the Hebrew midwives, of which the name of the one was Shiphrah, and the name of the other Puah:

וַיֹּאמֶר בְּיַלֶּדְכֶן אֶת־הָעִבְרִיּוֹת
and he said in your child birthing that - the Hebrew women

וּרְאִיתֶן עַל־הָאָבְנָיִם אִם־בֵּן הוּא וַהֲמִתֶּן אֹתוֹ
and you see the stones - upon if - son he and the you kill to him

וְאִם־בַּת הִוא וָחָיָה:
and if - daughter she and she lives

16 And he said, When ye do the office of a midwife to the Hebrew women, and see them upon the stools; if it be a son, then ye shall kill him: but if it be a daughter, then she shall live.

וַתִּירֶאןָ הַמְיַלְּדֹת אֶת־הָאֱלֹהִים
and they feared the midwives that - the Elohim

וְלֹא עָשׂוּ כַּאֲשֶׁר דִּבֶּר אֲלֵיהֶן מֶלֶךְ מִצְרָיִם
and not they did when spoke unto them king Egypt

וַתְּחַיֶּיןָ אֶת־הַיְלָדִים:
and they let live the boys - that

17 But the midwives feared God, and did not as the king of Egypt commanded them, but saved the men children alive.

[שני]

וַיִּקְרָא מֶלֶךְ־מִצְרַיִם לַמְיַלְּדֹת
and he called king - Egypt to midwives

PARASHAT 1   CHAPTER 1

וַיֹּאמֶר לָהֶן מַדּוּעַ עֲשִׂיתֶן הַדָּבָר הַזֶּה
the this the matter you did why to them and he said

וַתְּחַיֶּיןָ אֶת־הַיְלָדִים׃
the boys - that you let live

18 And the king of Egypt called for the midwives, and said unto them, Why have ye done this thing, and have saved the men children alive?

וַתֹּאמַרְןָ הַמְיַלְּדֹת אֶל־פַּרְעֹה
Pharaoh - unto the midwives and they answered

כִּי לֹא כַנָּשִׁים הַמִּצְרִיֹּת הָעִבְרִיֹּת
the Hebrews women the Egyptian women like woman not like

כִּי־חָיוֹת הֵנָּה בְּטֶרֶם תָּבוֹא אֲלֵהֶן הַמְיַלֶּדֶת וְיָלָדוּ׃
and they gave birth the midwives unto them she comes in before they are lively ones - like

19 And the midwives said unto Pharaoh, Because the Hebrew women are not as the Egyptian women; for they are lively, and are delivered ere the midwives come in unto them.

וַיֵּיטֶב אֱלֹהִים לַמְיַלְּדֹת
to midwives Elohim and he dealt good

וַיִּרֶב הָעָם וַיַּעַצְמוּ מְאֹד׃
greatly and they mightier the people and he increased

20 Therefore God dealt well with the midwives: and the people multiplied, and waxed very mighty.

וַיְהִי כִּי־יָרְאוּ הַמְיַלְּדֹת אֶת־הָאֱלֹהִים
the Elohim - that the midwives they feared - like and it was

וַיַּעַשׂ לָהֶם בָּתִּים׃
houses to them and he made

21 And it came to pass, because the midwives feared God, that he made them houses.

וַיְצַו פַּרְעֹה לְכָל־עַמּוֹ לֵאמֹר
to say his people - to all Pharaoh and he ordered

כָּל־הַבֵּן הַיִּלּוֹד הַיְאֹרָה תַּשְׁלִיכֻהוּ וְכָל־הַבַּת תְּחַיּוּן׃
you let live the daughter- and all you will cast him the towards river the born the son - all

22 And Pharaoh charged all his people, saying, Every son that is born ye shall cast into the river, and every daughter ye shall save alive.

פ

Chapter 2

ספר שמות פרק ב

וַיֵּלֶךְ אִישׁ מִבֵּית לֵוִי וַיִּקַּח אֶת־בַּת־לֵוִי׃
Levi - daughter - that   and he took   Levi   from house   man   and he went

1 And there went a man of the house of Levi, and took to wife a daughter of Levi.

וַתַּהַר הָאִשָּׁה וַתֵּלֶד בֵּן וַתֵּרֶא אֹתוֹ כִּי־טוֹב הוּא
he   good - like   to him   and she saw   son   and she bore   the woman   and she conceived

וַתִּצְפְּנֵהוּ שְׁלֹשָׁה יְרָחִים׃
months   three   and she secluded him

2 And the woman conceived, and bare a son: and when she saw him that he was a goodly child, she hid him three months.

וְלֹא־יָכְלָה עוֹד הַצְּפִינוֹ וַתִּקַּח־לוֹ תֵּבַת גֹּמֶא
papyrus   arc   to him - and she took   the his seclude   still   she able - and not

וַתַּחְמְרָה בַחֵמָר וּבַזָּפֶת וַתָּשֶׂם בָּהּ אֶת־הַיֶּלֶד
the boy - that   in it   and she put   and in pitch   in tar   and she coated it

וַתָּשֶׂם בַּסּוּף עַל־שְׂפַת הַיְאֹר׃
the river   bank - upon   in end   and she put

3 And when she could not longer hide him, she took for him an ark of bulrushes, and daubed it with slime and with pitch, and put the child therein; and she laid it in the flags by the river's brink.

וַתֵּתַצַּב אֲחֹתוֹ מֵרָחֹק לְדֵעָה מַה־יֵּעָשֶׂה לוֹ׃
to him   it will do - what   to know   from far   his sister   and she stood

4 And his sister stood afar off, to wit what would be done to him.

וַתֵּרֶד בַּת־פַּרְעֹה לִרְחֹץ עַל־הַיְאֹר
the river - upon   to wash   Pharaoh - daughter   and she descended

וְנַעֲרֹתֶיהָ הֹלְכֹת עַל־יַד הַיְאֹר
the river   side - upon   walking   and her maidens

וַתֵּרֶא אֶת־הַתֵּבָה בְּתוֹךְ הַסּוּף
the end   among   the arc - that   and she saw

וַתִּשְׁלַח אֶת־אֲמָתָהּ וַתִּקָּחֶהָ׃
and she took it   her maid - that   and she sent

5 And the daughter of Pharaoh came down to wash herself at the river; and her maidens walked along by the river's side; and when she saw the ark among the flags, she sent her maid to fetch it.

וַתִּפְתַּח֙ וַתִּרְאֵ֣הוּ אֶת־הַיֶּ֔לֶד וְהִנֵּה־נַ֖עַר בֹּכֶ֑ה
and she opened   and she saw him   the boy - that   child - and here   crying

וַתַּחְמֹ֣ל עָלָ֔יו וַתֹּ֕אמֶר מִיַּלְדֵ֥י הָֽעִבְרִ֖ים זֶֽה׃
and she had compassion   upon him   and she said   from boys   the Hebrews   this

6 And when she had opened it, she saw the child: and, behold, the babe wept. And she had compassion on him, and said, This is one of the Hebrews' children.

וַתֹּ֣אמֶר אֲחֹתוֹ֮ אֶל־בַּת־פַּרְעֹה֒
and she said   his sister   unto – daughter - Pharaoh

הַאֵלֵ֗ךְ וְקָרָ֤אתִי לָךְ֙ אִשָּׁ֣ה מֵינֶ֔קֶת מִ֖ן הָעִבְרִיֹּ֑ת
the I go   and I call   to you   woman   nursing   from   the Hebrew women

וְתֵינִ֥ק לָ֖ךְ אֶת־הַיָּֽלֶד׃
and she nurse   to you   the boy - that

7 Then said his sister to Pharaoh's daughter, Shall I go and call to thee a nurse of the Hebrew women, that she may nurse the child for thee?

וַתֹּֽאמֶר־לָ֥הּ בַּת־פַּרְעֹ֖ה לֵ֑כִי וַתֵּ֙לֶךְ֙ הָֽעַלְמָ֔ה
and she said - to her   Pharaoh - daughter   go you   and she went   the maid

וַתִּקְרָ֖א אֶת־אֵ֥ם הַיָּֽלֶד׃
and she called   that - mother   the boy

8 And Pharaoh's daughter said to her, Go. And the maid went and called the child's mother.

וַתֹּ֧אמֶר לָ֣הּ בַּת־פַּרְעֹ֗ה הֵילִ֜יכִי אֶת־הַיֶּ֤לֶד הַזֶּה֙
and she said   to her   Pharaoh - daughter   cause to go you   the boy - that   the this

וְהֵינִקִ֣הוּ לִ֔י וַאֲנִ֖י אֶתֵּ֣ן אֶת־שְׂכָרֵ֑ךְ
and cause nurse him   to me   and I   I will give   your wage - that

וַתִּקַּ֧ח הָאִשָּׁ֛ה הַיֶּ֖לֶד וַתְּנִיקֵֽהוּ׃
and she took   the woman   the boy   and she nursed him

9 And Pharaoh's daughter said unto her, Take this child away, and nurse it for me, and I will give thee thy wages. And the woman took the child, and nursed it.

וַיִּגְדַּ֣ל הַיֶּ֗לֶד וַתְּבִאֵ֙הוּ֙ לְבַת־פַּרְעֹ֔ה
and he grew   the child   and she brought him   to daughter - Pharaoh

וַֽיְהִי־לָ֖הּ לְבֵ֑ן וַתִּקְרָ֤א שְׁמוֹ֙ מֹשֶׁ֔ה
and he was - to her   to son   and she called   his name   Moses

וַתֹּ֕אמֶר כִּ֥י מִן־הַמַּ֖יִם מְשִׁיתִֽהוּ׃
and she said   like   from - the waters   I drew out him

10 And the child grew, and she brought him unto Pharaoh's daughter, and he

became her son. And she called his name Moses: and she said, Because I drew him out of the water.

[שלישי]

וַיְהִי בַּיָּמִים הָהֵם וַיִּגְדַּל מֹשֶׁה
and he was in days the those and he grew Moses

וַיֵּצֵא אֶל־אֶחָיו וַיַּרְא בְּסִבְלֹתָם
and he went out his brothers - unto and he saw in their burdens

וַיַּרְא אִישׁ מִצְרִי מַכֶּה אִישׁ־עִבְרִי מֵאֶחָיו:
and he saw man Egyptian beating Hebrew - man from his brothers

11 And it came to pass in those days, when Moses was grown, that he went out unto his brethren, and looked on their burdens: and he spied an Egyptian smiting an Hebrew, one of his brethren.

וַיִּפֶן כֹּה וָכֹה
and he glanced thus and thus

וַיַּרְא כִּי אֵין אִישׁ
and he saw like isn't man

וַיַּךְ אֶת־הַמִּצְרִי וַיִּטְמְנֵהוּ בַּחוֹל:
and he killed the Egyptian - that and he buried him in sand

12 And he looked this way and that way, and when he saw that there was no man, he slew the Egyptian, and hid him in the sand.

וַיֵּצֵא בַּיּוֹם הַשֵּׁנִי וְהִנֵּה שְׁנֵי־אֲנָשִׁים עִבְרִים נִצִּים
and he went out in day the second and here men - two Hebrews fighting ones

וַיֹּאמֶר לָרָשָׁע לָמָּה תַכֶּה רֵעֶךָ:
and he said to bad one why you strike your neighbor

13 And when he went out the second day, behold, two men of the Hebrews strove together: and he said to him that did the wrong, Wherefore smitest thou thy fellow?

וַיֹּאמֶר מִי שָׂמְךָ לְאִישׁ שַׂר וְשֹׁפֵט עָלֵינוּ
and he said who put you to man officer and judge upon us

הַלְהָרְגֵנִי אַתָּה אֹמֵר כַּאֲשֶׁר הָרַגְתָּ אֶת־הַמִּצְרִי
the to kill me you said when killed you the Egyptian - that

וַיִּירָא מֹשֶׁה וַיֹּאמַר אָכֵן נוֹדַע הַדָּבָר:
and he was afraid Moses and he said certainly it known the matter

14 And he said, Who made thee a prince and a judge over us? intendest thou to kill me, as thou killedst the Egyptian? And Moses feared, and said, Surely this thing is known.

וַיִּשְׁמַע פַּרְעֹה אֶת־הַדָּבָר הַזֶּה וַיְבַקֵּשׁ לַהֲרֹג אֶת־מֹשֶׁה
Moses - that   to the kill   and he sought   the this   the matter - that   Pharaoh   and he heard

וַיִּבְרַח מֹשֶׁה מִפְּנֵי פַרְעֹה
Pharaoh   form face   Moses   and he fled

וַיֵּשֶׁב בְּאֶרֶץ־מִדְיָן וַיֵּשֶׁב עַל־הַבְּאֵר:
the well - upon   and he sat   Midian - in land   and he dwelt

15 Now when Pharaoh heard this thing, he sought to slay Moses. But Moses fled from the face of Pharaoh, and dwelt in the land of Midian: and he sat down by a well.

וּלְכֹהֵן מִדְיָן שֶׁבַע בָּנוֹת
daughters   seven   Midian   and to priest

וַתָּבֹאנָה וַתִּדְלֶנָה וַתְּמַלֶּאנָה
and she filled   and she drew   and she came

אֶת־הָרְהָטִים לְהַשְׁקוֹת צֹאן אֲבִיהֶן:
their father   sheep   to water   the troughs - that

16 Now the priest of Midian had seven daughters: and they came and drew water, and filled the troughs to water their father's flock.

וַיָּבֹאוּ הָרֹעִים וַיְגָרְשׁוּם
and they drove them away   the herding ones   and they came

וַיָּקָם מֹשֶׁה וַיּוֹשִׁעָן וַיַּשְׁקְ אֶת־צֹאנָם:
their flock - that   and he watered   and he saved them   Moses   and he got up

17 And the shepherds came and drove them away: but Moses stood up and helped them, and watered their flock.

וַתָּבֹאנָה אֶל־רְעוּאֵל אֲבִיהֶן
their father   Reuel - unto   and she came there

וַיֹּאמֶר מַדּוּעַ מִהַרְתֶּן בֹּא הַיּוֹם:
the day   come   you haste   why   and he said

18 And when they came to Reuel their father, he said, How is it that ye are come so soon today?

וַתֹּאמַרְןָ אִישׁ מִצְרִי הִצִּילָנוּ מִיַּד הָרֹעִים
the shepherd ones   from hand   rescued us   Egyptian   man   and she said

וְגַם־דָּלֹה דָלָה לָנוּ וַיַּשְׁקְ אֶת־הַצֹּאן:
the sheep - that   and he watered   to us   he drew   drew - and also

19 And they said, An Egyptian delivered us out of the hand of the shepherds, and also drew water enough for us, and watered the flock.

וַיֹּאמֶר אֶל־בְּנֹתָיו וְאַיּוֹ לָמָּה זֶּה עֲזַבְתֶּן אֶת־הָאִישׁ
the man - that   you left   this   why   and where him   his daughters– unto   and he said

30   PARASHAT 1   CHAPTER 2

$$\text{קְרֶאןָ לוֹ וְיֹאכַל לָחֶם:}$$
bread   and he eat   to him   call

20 And he said unto his daughters, And where is he? why is it that ye have left the man? call him, that he may eat bread.

$$\text{וַיּוֹאֶל מֹשֶׁה לָשֶׁבֶת אֶת־הָאִישׁ}$$
the man – that   to dwell   Moses   and he content

$$\text{וַיִּתֵּן אֶת־צִפֹּרָה בִתּוֹ לְמֹשֶׁה:}$$
to Moses   his daughter   Zipporah – that   and he gave

21 And Moses was content to dwell with the man: and he gave Moses Zipporah his daughter.

$$\text{וַתֵּלֶד בֵּן וַיִּקְרָא אֶת־שְׁמוֹ גֵּרְשֹׁם}$$
Gershom   his name – that   and he called   Son   and she bare

$$\text{כִּי אָמַר גֵּר הָיִיתִי בְּאֶרֶץ נָכְרִיָּה:}$$
strange   in land   I was   stranger   he said   like

22 And she bare him a son, and he called his name Gershom: for he said, I have been a stranger in a strange land.

פ

$$\text{וַיְהִי בַיָּמִים הָרַבִּים הָהֵם וַיָּמָת מֶלֶךְ מִצְרַיִם}$$
Egypt   king   and he died   the them   the many ones   in days   and it was

$$\text{וַיֵּאָנְחוּ בְנֵי־יִשְׂרָאֵל מִן־הָעֲבֹדָה וַיִּזְעָקוּ}$$
and they cried out   the work – from   Israel – sons   and they sighed

$$\text{וַתַּעַל שַׁוְעָתָם אֶל־הָאֱלֹהִים מִן־הָעֲבֹדָה:}$$
the work – from   the Elohim – unto   their imploring   and it ascended

23 And it came to pass in process of time, that the king of Egypt died: and the children of Israel sighed by reason of the bondage, and they cried, and their cry came up unto God by reason of the bondage.

$$\text{וַיִּשְׁמַע אֱלֹהִים אֶת־נַאֲקָתָם}$$
their groaning – that   Elohim   and he heard

$$\text{וַיִּזְכֹּר אֱלֹהִים אֶת־בְּרִיתוֹ}$$
his covenant – that   Elohim   and he remembered

$$\text{אֶת־אַבְרָהָם אֶת־יִצְחָק וְאֶת־יַעֲקֹב:}$$
Jacob – and that   Isaac – that   Abraham – that

24 And God heard their groaning, and God remembered his covenant with Abraham, with Isaac, and with Jacob.

$$\text{וַיַּרְא אֱלֹהִים אֶת־בְּנֵי יִשְׂרָאֵל וַיֵּדַע אֱלֹהִים:}$$
Elohim   and he knowing   Israel   sons - that   Elohim   and he saw

25 And God looked upon the children of Israel, and God had respect unto

them.

ס

Chapter 3

ספר שמות פרק ג
[רביעי]

וּמֹשֶׁה הָיָה רֹעֶה אֶת־צֹאן יִתְרוֹ חֹתְנוֹ כֹּהֵן מִדְיָן
Midian Cohen his father in law Jethro flock - that shepherd was and Moses

וַיִּנְהַג אֶת־הַצֹּאן אַחַר הַמִּדְבָּר
the wilderness back the flock – that and he led

וַיָּבֹא אֶל־הַר הָאֱלֹהִים חֹרֵבָה:
towards Horeb the Elohim mountain – unto and he came

1 Now Moses kept the flock of Jethro his father in law, the priest of Midian: and he led the flock to the backside of the desert, and came to the mountain of God, even to Horeb.

וַיֵּרָא מַלְאַךְ יְהֹוָה אֵלָיו בְּלַבַּת־אֵשׁ מִתּוֹךְ הַסְּנֶה
the bush midst fire – in flame unto him ihvh angel and he appeared

וַיַּרְא וְהִנֵּה הַסְּנֶה בֹּעֵר בָּאֵשׁ
in fire burner the bush and here and he saw

וְהַסְּנֶה אֵינֶנּוּ אֻכָּל:
consumed isn't and the bush

2 And the angel of the LORD appeared unto him in a flame of fire out of the midst of a bush: and he looked, and, behold, the bush burned with fire, and the bush was not consumed.

וַיֹּאמֶר מֹשֶׁה אָסֻרָה־נָּא
now – I will turn aside Moshe and he said

וְאֶרְאֶה אֶת־הַמַּרְאֶה הַגָּדֹל הַזֶּה מַדּוּעַ לֹא־יִבְעַר הַסְּנֶה:
the bush it burn – not why the this the big the sight – that and I see

3 And Moses said, I will now turn aside, and see this great sight, why the bush is not burnt.

וַיַּרְא יְהֹוָה כִּי סָר לִרְאוֹת
to see turned like ihvh and he saw

וַיִּקְרָא אֵלָיו אֱלֹהִים מִתּוֹךְ הַסְּנֶה
the bush from midst Elohim unto him and he called

וַיֹּאמֶר מֹשֶׁה מֹשֶׁה
Moses Moses and he said

וַיֹּאמֶר הִנֵּנִי׃

here am I	and he said

4 And when the LORD saw that he turned aside to see, God called unto him out of the midst of the bush, and said, Moses, Moses. And he said, Here am I.

וַיֹּאמֶר אַל־תִּקְרַב הֲלֹם שַׁל־נְעָלֶיךָ מֵעַל רַגְלֶיךָ

| your feet | from upon | your sandal - ease off | hither | you near - don't | and he said |

כִּי הַמָּקוֹם אֲשֶׁר אַתָּה עוֹמֵד עָלָיו אַדְמַת־קֹדֶשׁ הוּא׃

| it | holy – ground | upon it | stand | you | which | the place | like |

5 And he said, Draw not nigh hither: put off thy shoes from off thy feet, for the place whereon thou standest is holy ground.

וַיֹּאמֶר אָנֹכִי אֱלֹהֵי אָבִיךָ

| your father | Elohim | I am | and he said |

אֱלֹהֵי אַבְרָהָם אֱלֹהֵי יִצְחָק וֵאלֹהֵי יַעֲקֹב

| Jacob | and Elohim | Isaac | Elohim | Abraham | Elohim |

וַיַּסְתֵּר מֹשֶׁה פָּנָיו כִּי יָרֵא מֵהַבִּיט אֶל־הָאֱלֹהִים׃

| the Elohim – unto | from beholding | he feared | like | his face | Moses | and he hid |

6 Moreover he said, I am the God of thy father, the God of Abraham, the God of Isaac, and the God of Jacob. And Moses hid his face; for he was afraid to look upon God.

וַיֹּאמֶר יְהוָה רָאֹה רָאִיתִי אֶת־עֳנִי עַמִּי אֲשֶׁר בְּמִצְרָיִם

| in Egypt | which | my people | affliction – that | I see | to see | ihvh | and he said |

וְאֶת־צַעֲקָתָם שָׁמַעְתִּי מִפְּנֵי נֹגְשָׂיו

| his task drivers | from face | I heard | their cry - and that |

כִּי יָדַעְתִּי אֶת־מַכְאֹבָיו׃

| his suffering – that | I know | like |

7 And the LORD said, I have surely seen the affliction of my people which are in Egypt, and have heard their cry by reason of their taskmasters; for I know their sorrows;

וָאֵרֵד לְהַצִּילוֹ מִיַּד מִצְרַיִם

| Egyptians | from hand | to deliver him | and I came down |

וּלְהַעֲלֹתוֹ מִן־הָאָרֶץ הַהִוא אֶל־אֶרֶץ טוֹבָה וּרְחָבָה

| and wide | good | land – unto | the it | the land – from | and to the his ascending |

אֶל־אֶרֶץ זָבַת חָלָב וּדְבָשׁ אֶל־מְקוֹם הַכְּנַעֲנִי

| the Canaanites | place – unto | and honey | milk | flowing | land – unto |

וְהַחִתִּי וְהָאֱמֹרִי וְהַפְּרִזִּי וְהַחִוִּי וְהַיְבוּסִי׃

| and the Jebusites | and the Hivites | and the Perizzites | and the Amorites | and the Hittites |

8 And I am come down to deliver them out of the hand of the Egyptians, and to bring them up out of that land unto a good land and a large, unto a land flowing with milk and honey; unto the place of the Canaanites, and the Hittites, and the Amorites, and the Perizzites, and the Hivites, and the Jebusites.

וְעַתָּה הִנֵּה צַעֲקַת בְּנֵי־יִשְׂרָאֵל בָּאָה אֵלָי
and now   and   cry   sons - Israel   come   unto me

וְגַם־רָאִיתִי אֶת־הַלַּחַץ אֲשֶׁר מִצְרַיִם לֹחֲצִים אֹתָם׃
I saw - and also   the oppression – that   Egyptians   oppressing ones   to them

9 Now therefore, behold, the cry of the children of Israel is come unto me: and I have also seen the oppression wherewith the Egyptians oppress them.

וְעַתָּה לְכָה וְאֶשְׁלָחֲךָ אֶל־פַּרְעֹה
and now   go   and I will send you   Pharaoh – unto

וְהוֹצֵא אֶת־עַמִּי בְנֵי־יִשְׂרָאֵל מִמִּצְרָיִם׃
and bring out   my people – that   sons – Israel   from Egypt

10 Come now therefore, and I will send thee unto Pharaoh, that thou mayest bring forth my people the children of Israel out of Egypt.

וַיֹּאמֶר מֹשֶׁה אֶל־הָאֱלֹהִים מִי אָנֹכִי כִּי אֵלֵךְ אֶל־פַּרְעֹה
and he said   Moses   the Elohim – unto   who   I am   like   I go   Pharaoh – unto

וְכִי אוֹצִיא אֶת־בְּנֵי יִשְׂרָאֵל מִמִּצְרָיִם׃
and like   I bring out   sons – that   Israel   from Egypt

11 And Moses said unto God, Who am I, that I should go unto Pharaoh, and that I should bring forth the children of Israel out of Egypt?

וַיֹּאמֶר כִּי־אֶהְיֶה עִמָּךְ וְזֶה־לְּךָ הָאוֹת
and he said   I will be - like   with you   and this – to you   the sign

כִּי אָנֹכִי שְׁלַחְתִּיךָ בְּהוֹצִיאֲךָ אֶת־הָעָם מִמִּצְרַיִם
like   I am   sending you   in your bringing out   the people - that   from Egypt

תַּעַבְדוּן אֶת־הָאֱלֹהִים עַל הָהָר הַזֶּה׃
you will serve   the Elohim – that   upon   the mountain   the this

12 And he said, Certainly I will be with thee; and this shall be a token unto thee, that I have sent thee: When thou hast brought forth the people out of Egypt, ye shall serve God upon this mountain.

וַיֹּאמֶר מֹשֶׁה אֶל־הָאֱלֹהִים
and he said   Moses   the Elohim – unto

הִנֵּה אָנֹכִי בָא אֶל־בְּנֵי יִשְׂרָאֵל
here   I am   come   sons – unto   Israel

וְאָמַרְתִּי לָהֶם אֱלֹהֵי אֲבוֹתֵיכֶם שְׁלָחַנִי אֲלֵיכֶם
and I said   to them   Elohim   your fathers   sent me   unto you

PARASHAT 1 CHAPTER 3

וְאָמְרוּ־לִ֣י מַה־שְּׁמ֔וֹ מָ֥ה אֹמַ֖ר אֲלֵהֶֽם׃
unto them   I will say   what   his name – what   to me – and they will say

13 And Moses said unto God, Behold, when I come unto the children of Israel, and shall say unto them, The God of your fathers hath sent me unto you; and they shall say to me, What is his name? what shall I say unto them?

וַיֹּ֤אמֶר אֱלֹהִים֙ אֶל־מֹשֶׁ֔ה אֶֽהְיֶ֖ה אֲשֶׁ֣ר אֶֽהְיֶ֑ה
I am   which   I am   Moses – unto   Elohim   and he said

וַיֹּ֗אמֶר כֹּ֤ה תֹאמַר֙ לִבְנֵ֣י יִשְׂרָאֵ֔ל אֶֽהְיֶ֖ה שְׁלָחַ֥נִי אֲלֵיכֶֽם׃
unto you   sent me   I am   Israel   to sons   you will say   thus   and he said

14 And God said unto Moses, I AM THAT I AM: and he said, Thus shalt thou say unto the children of Israel, I AM hath sent me unto you.

וַיֹּאמֶר֩ ע֨וֹד אֱלֹהִ֜ים אֶל־מֹשֶׁ֗ה כֹּֽה־תֹאמַר֮ אֶל־בְּנֵ֣י יִשְׂרָאֵל֒
Israel   sons - unto   you will say   thus   Moses – unto   Elohim   again   and he said

יְהוָ֞ה אֱלֹהֵ֣י אֲבֹתֵיכֶ֗ם
your fathers   Elohim   ihvh

אֱלֹהֵ֧י אַבְרָהָ֛ם אֱלֹהֵ֥י יִצְחָ֖ק וֵֽאלֹהֵ֣י יַעֲקֹ֑ב
Jacob   and Elohim   Isaac   Elohim   Abraham   Elohim

שְׁלָחַ֣נִי אֲלֵיכֶ֑ם זֶה־שְּׁמִ֣י לְעֹלָ֔ם
to forever   my name – this   unto you   sent me

וְזֶ֥ה זִכְרִ֖י לְדֹ֥ר דֹּֽר׃
generation   to generation   memorial   and this

15 And God said moreover unto Moses, Thus shalt thou say unto the children of Israel, The LORD God of your fathers, the God of Abraham, the God of Isaac, and the God of Jacob, hath sent me unto you: this is my name for ever, and this is my memorial unto all generations.

[חמישי]

לֵ֣ךְ וְאָֽסַפְתָּ֞ אֶת־זִקְנֵ֣י יִשְׂרָאֵ֗ל
Israel   elders - that   and you gather   go

וְאָמַרְתָּ֤ אֲלֵהֶם֙ יְהוָ֞ה אֱלֹהֵ֤י אֲבֹֽתֵיכֶם֙ נִרְאָ֣ה אֵלַ֔י
unto me   appeared   your fathers   Elohim   ihvh   unto them   and you say

אֱלֹהֵ֧י אַבְרָהָ֛ם יִצְחָ֥ק וְיַעֲקֹ֖ב לֵאמֹ֑ר
to say   and Jacob   Isaac   Abraham   Elohim

פָּקֹ֤ד פָּקַ֨דְתִּי֙ אֶתְכֶ֔ם וְאֶת־הֶעָשׂ֥וּי לָכֶ֖ם בְּמִצְרָֽיִם׃
in Egypt   to you   the being done - and that   that you   I visited   visiter

16 Go, and gather the elders of Israel together, and say unto them, The LORD God of your fathers, the God of Abraham, of Isaac, and of Jacob, appeared unto me, saying, I have surely visited you, and seen that which is done to you

in Egypt:

וָאֹמַ֗ר אַעֲלֶ֣ה אֶתְכֶם֮ מֵעֳנִ֣י מִצְרַ֒יִם֒ אֶל־אֶ֤רֶץ הַֽכְּנַעֲנִי֙
and I said I will bring up that you from affliction Egypt land - unto the Canaanites

וְהַ֣חִתִּ֔י וְהָֽאֱמֹרִי֙ וְהַפְּרִזִּ֔י וְהַחִוִּ֖י וְהַיְבוּסִ֑י
and the Hittiltes and the Amorites and the Perizzites and the Hivites and the Jebusites

אֶל־אֶ֛רֶץ זָבַ֥ת חָלָ֖ב וּדְבָֽשׁ׃
unto- land flowing milk and honey

17 And I have said, I will bring you up out of the affliction of Egypt unto the land of the Canaanites, and the Hittites, and the Amorites, and the Perizzites, and the Hivites, and the Jebusites, unto a land flowing with milk and honey.

וְשָׁמְע֖וּ לְקֹלֶ֑ךָ
and they will listen to your voice

וּבָאתָ֡ אַתָּה֩ וְזִקְנֵ֨י יִשְׂרָאֵ֜ל אֶל־מֶ֣לֶךְ מִצְרַ֗יִם
and you will come you and elders Israel unto - king Egypt

וַאֲמַרְתֶּ֤ם אֵלָיו֙ יְהוָ֞ה אֱלֹהֵ֤י הָֽעִבְרִיִּים֙ נִקְרָ֣ה עָלֵ֔ינוּ
and you will say unto him ihvh Elohim the Hebrews met upon us

וְעַתָּ֗ה נֵֽלֲכָה־נָּ֞א דֶּ֣רֶךְ שְׁלֹ֤שֶׁת יָמִים֙ בַּמִּדְבָּ֔ר
and now now - we go way three days in wilderness

וְנִזְבְּחָ֖ה לַֽיהוָ֥ה אֱלֹהֵֽינוּ׃
and we sacrifice to ihvh our Elohim

18 And they shall hearken to thy voice: and thou shalt come, thou and the elders of Israel, unto the king of Egypt, and ye shall say unto him, The LORD God of the Hebrews hath met with us: and now let us go, we beseech thee, three days' journey into the wilderness, that we may sacrifice to the LORD our God.

וַאֲנִ֣י יָדַ֔עְתִּי כִּ֠י לֹֽא־יִתֵּ֥ן אֶתְכֶ֛ם מֶ֥לֶךְ מִצְרַ֖יִם לַהֲלֹ֑ךְ
and I I know like he will give - not that you king Egypt to go

וְלֹ֖א בְּיָ֥ד חֲזָקָֽה׃
and not in hand mighty

19 And I am sure that the king of Egypt will not let you go, no, not by a mighty hand.

וְשָׁלַחְתִּ֤י אֶת־יָדִי֙ וְהִכֵּיתִ֣י אֶת־מִצְרַ֔יִם בְּכֹל֙ נִפְלְאֹתַ֔י
and I will send out my hand - that and I will strike Egypt - that in all my wonders

אֲשֶׁ֥ר אֶֽעֱשֶׂ֖ה בְּקִרְבּ֑וֹ וְאַחֲרֵי־כֵ֖ן יְשַׁלַּ֥ח אֶתְכֶֽם׃
which I will do in his midst thus - and after he will send that you

20 And I will stretch out my hand, and smite Egypt with all my wonders which I will do in the midst thereof: and after that he will let you go.

וְנָתַתִּ֞י אֶת־חֵ֥ן הָעָם־הַזֶּ֖ה בְּעֵינֵ֣י מִצְרָ֑יִם
and I will give - that grace   the this - the people   in eyes   Egyptians

וְהָיָה֙ כִּ֣י תֵֽלֵכ֔וּן לֹ֥א תֵלְכ֖וּ רֵיקָֽם׃
and it will be   like   when you will go   not   you will go   empty

21 And I will give this people favour in the sight of the Egyptians: and it shall come to pass, that, when ye go, ye shall not go empty:

וְשָׁאֲלָ֨ה אִשָּׁ֤ה מִשְּׁכֶנְתָּהּ֙ וּמִגָּרַ֣ת בֵּיתָ֔הּ
and she will ask   woman   from her close dweller   and from one sojourning   her house

כְּלֵי־כֶ֛סֶף וּכְלֵ֥י זָהָ֖ב וּשְׂמָלֹ֑ת
silver - articles   and articles   gold   and garments

וְשַׂמְתֶּ֗ם עַל־בְּנֵיכֶם֙ וְעַל־בְּנֹ֣תֵיכֶ֔ם
and you will put them   upon - your sons   and upon - your daughters

וְנִצַּלְתֶּ֖ם אֶת־מִצְרָֽיִם׃
and you will plunder them   that - Egyptians

22 But every woman shall borrow of her neighbour, and of her that sojourneth in her house, jewels of silver, and jewels of gold, and raiment: and ye shall put them upon your sons, and upon your daughters; and ye shall spoil the Egyptians.

Chapter 4

ספר שמות פרק ד

וַיַּ֤עַן מֹשֶׁה֙ וַיֹּ֔אמֶר וְהֵן֙ לֹֽא־יַאֲמִ֣ינוּ לִ֔י
and he answered   Moses   and he said   and thus   not - they will believe   to me

וְלֹ֥א יִשְׁמְע֖וּ בְּקֹלִ֑י כִּ֣י יֹֽאמְר֔וּ לֹֽא־נִרְאָ֥ה אֵלֶ֖יךָ יְהוָֽה׃
and not   they will listen   in my voice   like   they will say   not - appeared   unto you   ihvh

1 And Moses answered and said, But, behold, they will not believe me, nor hearken unto my voice: for they will say, The LORD hath not appeared unto thee.

וַיֹּ֧אמֶר אֵלָ֛יו יְהוָ֖ה [מַה־זֶּ֣ה] בְיָדֶ֑ךָ
and he said   unto him   ihvh   what - this   in your hand

וַיֹּ֖אמֶר מַטֶּֽה׃
and he said   staff

2 And the LORD said unto him, What is that in thine hand? And he said, A rod.

וַיֹּ֨אמֶר֙ הַשְׁלִיכֵ֣הוּ אַ֔רְצָה וַיַּשְׁלִכֵ֥הוּ אַ֖רְצָה
and he said   the throw it   towards ground   and he threw it   towards ground

וַיְהִ֣י לְנָחָ֑שׁ וַיָּ֥נָס מֹשֶׁ֖ה מִפָּנָֽיו׃
and it became   to snake   and he fled   Moses   from before it

Parashat 1   Chapter 4   37

3 And he said, Cast it on the ground. And he cast it on the ground, and it became a serpent; and Moses fled from before it.

וַיֹּאמֶר יְהוָה אֶל־מֹשֶׁה שְׁלַח יָדְךָ וֶאֱחֹז בִּזְנָבוֹ
and he said ihvh Moses - unto throw out your hand and catch in it's tail

וַיִּשְׁלַח יָדוֹ וַיַּחֲזֶק־בּוֹ
and he threw out his hand and he grabbed - in it

וַיְהִי לְמַטֶּה בְּכַפּוֹ׃
and it was to staff in his palm

4 And the LORD said unto Moses, Put forth thine hand, and take it by the tail. And he put forth his hand, and caught it, and it became a rod in his hand:

לְמַעַן יַאֲמִינוּ
to end they will believe

כִּי־נִרְאָה אֵלֶיךָ יְהוָה אֱלֹהֵי אֲבֹתָם
like - he appeared unto you ihvh Elohim their fathers

אֱלֹהֵי אַבְרָהָם אֱלֹהֵי יִצְחָק וֵאלֹהֵי יַעֲקֹב׃
Elohim Abraham Elohim Isaac and Elohim Jacob

5 That they may believe that the LORD God of their fathers, the God of Abraham, the God of Isaac, and the God of Jacob, hath appeared unto thee.

וַיֹּאמֶר יְהוָה לוֹ עוֹד הָבֵא־נָא יָדְךָ בְּחֵיקֶךָ
and he said ihvh to him again bring the - now your hand in your bosom

וַיָּבֵא יָדוֹ בְּחֵיקוֹ
and he brought his hand in his bosom

וַיּוֹצִאָהּ וְהִנֵּה יָדוֹ מְצֹרַעַת כַּשָּׁלֶג׃
and he come out it and here his hand from leprosy like snow

6 And the LORD said furthermore unto him, Put now thine hand into thy bosom. And he put his hand into his bosom: and when he took it out, behold, his hand was leprous as snow.

וַיֹּאמֶר הָשֵׁב יָדְךָ אֶל־חֵיקֶךָ
and he said the return you're hand unto - your bosom

וַיָּשֶׁב יָדוֹ אֶל־חֵיקוֹ
and he returned his hand unto - his bosom

וַיּוֹצִאָהּ מֵחֵיקוֹ וְהִנֵּה־שָׁבָה כִּבְשָׂרוֹ׃
and he came out from his bosom and here - returned like his flesh

7 And he said, Put thine hand into thy bosom again. And he put his hand into his bosom again; and plucked it out of his bosom, and, behold, it was turned again as his other flesh.

וְהָיָה אִם־לֹא יַאֲמִינוּ לָךְ
to you they will believe not - if and it will be

וְלֹא יִשְׁמְעוּ לְקֹל הָאֹת הָרִאשׁוֹן
the first the sign to voice they will hear and not

וְהֶאֱמִינוּ לְקֹל הָאֹת הָאַחֲרוֹן׃
the following the sign to voice and the they will believe

8 And it shall come to pass, if they will not believe thee, neither hearken to the voice of the first sign, that they will believe the voice of the latter sign.

וְהָיָה אִם־לֹא יַאֲמִינוּ גַּם לִשְׁנֵי הָאֹתוֹת הָאֵלֶּה
the these the signs to two also they will believe not - if and it will be

וְלֹא יִשְׁמְעוּן לְקֹלֶךָ וְלָקַחְתָּ מִמֵּימֵי הַיְאֹר
the river from waters and you will take to your voice they will hear and not

וְשָׁפַכְתָּ הַיַּבָּשָׁה וְהָיוּ הַמַּיִם אֲשֶׁר תִּקַּח מִן־הַיְאֹר
the river - from you take which the waters and it will become the dry land and you pour

וְהָיוּ לְדָם בַּיַּבָּשֶׁת׃
in dry lands to blood and it will become

9 And it shall come to pass, if they will not believe also these two signs, neither hearken unto thy voice, that thou shalt take of the water of the river, and pour it upon the dry land: and the water which thou takest out of the river shall become blood upon the dry land.

וַיֹּאמֶר מֹשֶׁה אֶל־יְהֹוָה בִּי אֲדֹנָי לֹא אִישׁ דְּבָרִים אָנֹכִי
I am speakings man not Adoni in me ihvh - unto Moses and he said

גַּם מִתְּמוֹל גַּם מִשִּׁלְשֹׁם גַּם מֵאָז דַּבֶּרְךָ אֶל־עַבְדֶּךָ
your servant - unto your speech from ear also from thee days also yesterday also

כִּי כְבַד־פֶּה וּכְבַד לָשׁוֹן אָנֹכִי׃
I am tongue and heavy mouth - heavy like

10 And Moses said unto the LORD, O my Lord, I am not eloquent, neither heretofore, nor since thou hast spoken unto thy servant: but I am slow of speech, and of a slow tongue.

וַיֹּאמֶר יְהֹוָה אֵלָיו מִי שָׂם פֶּה לָאָדָם אוֹ
or to Adam mouth put who unto him ihvh and he said

מִי־יָשׂוּם אִלֵּם אוֹ חֵרֵשׁ אוֹ פִקֵּחַ אוֹ עִוֵּר
blind or sight or deaf or mute he places - who

הֲלֹא אָנֹכִי יְהֹוָה׃
ihvh I am the not

11 And the LORD said unto him, Who hath made man's mouth? or who maketh the dumb, or deaf, or the seeing, or the blind? have not I the LORD?

PARASHAT 1   CHAPTER 4

וְעַתָּ֣ה לֵ֔ךְ וְאָנֹכִי֙ אֶֽהְיֶ֣ה עִם־פִּ֔יךָ
your mouth - with   I will be   and I am   go   and now

וְהוֹרֵיתִ֖יךָ אֲשֶׁ֥ר תְּדַבֵּֽר׃
you will say   which   and I will teach you

12 Now therefore go, and I will be with thy mouth, and teach thee what thou shalt say.

וַיֹּ֖אמֶר בִּ֣י אֲדֹנָ֑י שְֽׁלַֽח־נָ֖א בְּיַד־תִּשְׁלָֽח׃
you will send - in hand   now - send   Adoni   in me   and he said

13 And he said, O my Lord, send, I pray thee, by the hand of him whom thou wilt send.

וַיִּֽחַר־אַ֨ף יְהֹוָ֜ה בְּמֹשֶׁ֗ה וַיֹּ֨אמֶר֙
and he said   in Moses   ihvh   anger - and he kindled

הֲלֹ֨א אַהֲרֹ֤ן אָחִ֨יךָ֙ הַלֵּוִ֔י יָדַ֕עְתִּי כִּֽי־דַבֵּ֥ר יְדַבֵּ֖ר ה֑וּא
he   he speaks   speak - like   I know   the Levite   your brother   Aaron   the not

וְגַ֤ם הִנֵּה־הוּא֙ יֹצֵ֣א לִקְרָאתֶ֔ךָ וְרָאֲךָ֖ וְשָׂמַ֥ח בְּלִבּֽוֹ׃
in his heart   and he will be glad   and he sees you   to meet you   coming out   he - here   and also

14 And the anger of the LORD was kindled against Moses, and he said, Is not Aaron the Levite thy brother? I know that he can speak well. And also, behold, he cometh forth to meet thee: and when he seeth thee, he will be glad in his heart.

וְדִבַּרְתָּ֣ אֵלָ֔יו וְשַׂמְתָּ֥ אֶת־הַדְּבָרִ֖ים בְּפִ֑יו
in his mouth   the speakings - that   and you will put   unto him   and you will speak

וְאָנֹכִ֗י אֶֽהְיֶ֤ה עִם־פִּ֨יךָ֙ וְעִם־פִּ֔יהוּ
his mouth - and with   mouth your - with   will be   and I am

וְהוֹרֵיתִ֣י אֶתְכֶ֔ם אֵ֖ת אֲשֶׁ֥ר תַּעֲשֽׂוּן׃
you will do   which   that   that you   and I will teach

15 And thou shalt speak unto him, and put words in his mouth: and I will be with thy mouth, and with his mouth, and will teach you what ye shall do.

וְדִבֶּר־ה֥וּא לְךָ֖ אֶל־הָעָ֑ם וְהָ֣יָה
and he will be   the people - unto   to you   he - and will speak

ה֤וּא יִֽהְיֶה־לְּךָ֙ לְפֶ֔ה וְאַתָּ֖ה תִּֽהְיֶה־לּ֥וֹ לֵֽאלֹהִֽים׃
to Elohim   to him - you will be   and you   to mouth   to you - he will be   he

16 And he shall be thy spokesman unto the people: and he shall be, even he shall be to thee instead of a mouth, and thou shalt be to him instead of God.

וְאֶת־הַמַּטֶּ֥ה הַזֶּ֖ה תִּקַּ֣ח בְּיָדֶ֑ךָ
in your hand   you will take   the this   the staff - and that

אֲשֶׁ֥ר תַּעֲשֶׂה־בּ֖וֹ אֶת־הָאֹתֹֽת׃
which   you will do - in it   that - the sign

17 And thou shalt take this rod in thine hand, wherewith thou shalt do signs.

פ

[שׁשׁי]

וַיֵּ֣לֶךְ מֹשֶׁ֗ה וַיָּ֨שָׁב֙ אֶל־יֶ֣תֶר חֹֽתְנ֔וֹ
and he went Moses and he returned unto - Jether his father in law

וַיֹּ֣אמֶר ל֗וֹ אֵ֣לְכָה נָּ֗א וְאָשׁ֨וּבָה֙ אֶל־אַחַ֣י אֲשֶׁר־בְּמִצְרַ֔יִם
and he said to him I go - now and I return unto - my brothers which - in Egypt

וְאֶרְאֶ֖ה הַעוֹדָ֣ם חַיִּ֑ים
and I see the still them alive ones

וַיֹּ֧אמֶר יִתְר֛וֹ לְמֹשֶׁ֖ה לֵ֥ךְ לְשָׁלֽוֹם׃
and he said Jethro to Moses go to peace

18 And Moses went and returned to Jethro his father in law, and said unto him, Let me go, I pray thee, and return unto my brethren which are in Egypt, and see whether they be yet alive. And Jethro said to Moses, Go in peace.

וַיֹּ֨אמֶר יְהוָ֤ה אֶל־מֹשֶׁה֙ בְּמִדְיָ֔ן לֵ֖ךְ שֻׁ֣ב מִצְרָ֑יִם
and he said ihvh unto - Moses in Midian go return Egypt

כִּי־מֵ֨תוּ֙ כָּל־הָ֣אֲנָשִׁ֔ים הַֽמְבַקְשִׁ֖ים אֶת־נַפְשֶֽׁךָ׃
they died - like all - the men the seeker ones that - your soul

19 And the LORD said unto Moses in Midian, Go, return into Egypt: for all the men are dead which sought thy life.

וַיִּקַּ֨ח מֹשֶׁ֜ה אֶת־אִשְׁתּ֣וֹ וְאֶת־בָּנָ֗יו וַיַּרְכִּבֵם֙ עַֽל־הַחֲמֹ֔ר
and he took Moses that - his wife and that - his sons upon - the donkey

וַיָּ֖שָׁב אַ֣רְצָה מִצְרָ֑יִם וַיַּרְכִּבֵ֑ם
and he returned towards land Egypt and he made ride them

וַיִּקַּ֥ח מֹשֶׁ֛ה אֶת־מַטֵּ֥ה הָאֱלֹהִ֖ים בְּיָדֽוֹ׃
and he took Moses that - staff the Elohim in his hand

20 And Moses took his wife and his sons, and set them upon an ass, and he returned to the land of Egypt: and Moses took the rod of God in his hand.

וַיֹּ֤אמֶר יְהוָה֙ אֶל־מֹשֶׁ֔ה בְּלֶכְתְּךָ֖ לָשׁ֣וּב מִצְרַ֑יְמָה
and he said ihvh unto - Moses in your going to return towards Egypt

רְאֵ֗ה כָּל־הַמֹּֽפְתִים֙ אֲשֶׁר־שַׂ֣מְתִּי בְיָדֶ֔ךָ
see all - the wonders which - I put in your hand

וַעֲשִׂיתָ֖ם לִפְנֵ֣י פַרְעֹ֑ה וַאֲנִי֙ אֲחַזֵּ֣ק אֶת־לִבּ֔וֹ
and you do them before Pharaoh and I I harden that - his heart

$$\underset{\text{and not}}{\text{וְלֹא}} \ \underset{\text{he will send}}{\text{יְשַׁלַּח}} \ \underset{\text{that - the people}}{\text{אֶת־הָעָם:}}$$

21 And the LORD said unto Moses, When thou goest to return into Egypt, see that thou do all those wonders before Pharaoh, which I have put in thine hand: but I will harden his heart, that he shall not let the people go.

$$\underset{\text{and you will say}}{\text{וְאָמַרְתָּ}} \ \underset{\text{Pharaoh - unto}}{\text{אֶל־פַּרְעֹה}} \ \underset{\text{thus}}{\text{כֹּה}} \ \underset{\text{say}}{\text{אָמַר}} \ \underset{\text{ihvh}}{\text{יְהוָה}} \ \underset{\text{my son}}{\text{בְּנִי}} \ \underset{\text{my firstborn}}{\text{בְכֹרִי}} \ \underset{\text{Israel}}{\text{יִשְׂרָאֵל:}}$$

22 And thou shalt say unto Pharaoh, Thus saith the LORD, Israel is my son, even my firstborn:

$$\underset{\text{and I say}}{\text{וָאֹמַר}} \ \underset{\text{unto you}}{\text{אֵלֶיךָ}} \ \underset{\text{send}}{\text{שַׁלַּח}} \ \underset{\text{my son - that}}{\text{אֶת־בְּנִי}} \ \underset{\text{and he serve me}}{\text{וְיַעַבְדֵנִי}}$$

$$\underset{\text{and you refuse}}{\text{וַתְּמָאֵן}} \ \underset{\text{to send him}}{\text{לְשַׁלְּחוֹ}} \ \underset{\text{here}}{\text{הִנֵּה}} \ \underset{\text{I am}}{\text{אָנֹכִי}} \ \underset{\text{killer}}{\text{הֹרֵג}} \ \underset{\text{your son - that}}{\text{אֶת־בִּנְךָ}} \ \underset{\text{your first born}}{\text{בְּכֹרֶךָ:}}$$

23 And I say unto thee, Let my son go, that he may serve me: and if thou refuse to let him go, behold, I will slay thy son, even thy firstborn.

$$\underset{\text{and it was}}{\text{וַיְהִי}} \ \underset{\text{in way}}{\text{בַדֶּרֶךְ}} \ \underset{\text{in inn}}{\text{בַּמָּלוֹן}} \ \underset{\text{and he met him}}{\text{וַיִּפְגְּשֵׁהוּ}} \ \underset{\text{ihvh}}{\text{יְהוָה}}$$

$$\underset{\text{and he sought}}{\text{וַיְבַקֵּשׁ}} \ \underset{\text{the his kill}}{\text{הֲמִיתוֹ:}}$$

24 And it came to pass by the way in the inn, that the LORD met him, and sought to kill him.

$$\underset{\text{and she took}}{\text{וַתִּקַּח}} \ \underset{\text{Zipporah}}{\text{צִפֹּרָה}} \ \underset{\text{flint knife}}{\text{צֹר}} \ \underset{\text{and she cut off}}{\text{וַתִּכְרֹת}} \ \underset{\text{foreskin - that}}{\text{אֶת־עָרְלַת}} \ \underset{\text{her son}}{\text{בְּנָהּ}}$$

$$\underset{\text{and she touched}}{\text{וַתַּגַּע}} \ \underset{\text{to his feet}}{\text{לְרַגְלָיו}} \ \underset{\text{and she said}}{\text{וַתֹּאמֶר}} \ \underset{\text{like}}{\text{כִּי}} \ \underset{\text{blood ones - bridegroom}}{\text{חֲתַן־דָּמִים}} \ \underset{\text{you}}{\text{אַתָּה}} \ \underset{\text{to me}}{\text{לִי:}}$$

25 Then Zipporah took a sharp stone, and cut off the foreskin of her son, and cast it at his feet, and said, Surely a bloody husband art thou to me.

$$\underset{\text{and he slacked}}{\text{וַיִּרֶף}} \ \underset{\text{from him}}{\text{מִמֶּנּוּ}} \ \underset{\text{then}}{\text{אָז}} \ \underset{\text{she said}}{\text{אָמְרָה}} \ \underset{\text{bridegroom}}{\text{חֲתַן}} \ \underset{\text{blood ones}}{\text{דָּמִים}} \ \underset{\text{to circumcision}}{\text{לַמּוּלֹת:}}$$

26 So he let him go: then she said, A bloody husband thou art, because of the circumcision.

פ

$$\underset{\text{and he said}}{\text{וַיֹּאמֶר}} \ \underset{\text{ihvh}}{\text{יְהוָה}} \ \underset{\text{Aaron - unto}}{\text{אֶל־אַהֲרֹן}} \ \underset{\text{go}}{\text{לֵךְ}} \ \underset{\text{to meet}}{\text{לִקְרַאת}} \ \underset{\text{Moses}}{\text{מֹשֶׁה}} \ \underset{\text{the towards wilderness}}{\text{הַמִּדְבָּרָה}}$$

$$\underset{\text{and he went}}{\text{וַיֵּלֶךְ}} \ \underset{\text{and he met him}}{\text{וַיִּפְגְּשֵׁהוּ}} \ \underset{\text{in mountain}}{\text{בְּהַר}} \ \underset{\text{the Elohim}}{\text{הָאֱלֹהִים}} \ \underset{\text{to him - and he kissed}}{\text{וַיִּשַּׁק־לוֹ:}}$$

27 And the LORD said to Aaron, Go into the wilderness to meet Moses. And he went, and met him in the mount of God, and kissed him.

וַיַּגֵּ֤ד מֹשֶׁה֙ לְאַהֲרֹ֔ן אֵ֥ת כׇּל־דִּבְרֵ֥י יְהֹוָ֖ה אֲשֶׁ֣ר שְׁלָח֑וֹ
sent him　which　ihvh　speakings - all　that　to Aaron　Moses　and he told

וְאֵ֥ת כׇּל־הָאֹתֹ֖ת אֲשֶׁ֥ר צִוָּֽהוּ׃
commanded him　which　the signs - all　and that

28 And Moses told Aaron all the words of the LORD who had sent him, and all the signs which he had commanded him.

וַיֵּ֥לֶךְ מֹשֶׁ֖ה וְאַהֲרֹ֑ן
and Aaron　Moses　and he went

וַיַּ֣אַסְפ֔וּ אֶת־כׇּל־זִקְנֵ֖י בְּנֵ֥י יִשְׂרָאֵֽל׃
Israel　sons　elders - all - that　and they gathered

29 And Moses and Aaron went and gathered together all the elders of the children of Israel:

וַיְדַבֵּ֣ר אַהֲרֹ֔ן אֵ֚ת כׇּל־הַדְּבָרִ֔ים אֲשֶׁר־דִּבֶּ֥ר יְהֹוָ֖ה אֶל־מֹשֶׁ֑ה
Moses - unto　ihvh　spoke - which　the speakings - all　that　Aaron　and he spoke

וַיַּ֥עַשׂ הָאֹתֹ֖ת לְעֵינֵ֥י הָעָֽם׃
the people　to eyes　the signs　and he did

30 And Aaron spake all the words which the LORD had spoken unto Moses, and did the signs in the sight of the people.

וַֽיַּאֲמֵ֖ן הָעָ֑ם
the people　and he believed

וַֽיִּשְׁמְע֡וּ כִּֽי־פָקַ֨ד יְהֹוָ֜ה אֶת־בְּנֵ֣י יִשְׂרָאֵ֗ל
Israel　sons - that　ihvh　visited – like　and they heard

וְכִ֤י רָאָה֙ אֶת־עׇנְיָ֔ם
their affliction - that　he saw　and like

וַֽיִּקְּד֖וּ וַיִּֽשְׁתַּחֲוֽוּ׃
and they bowed down　and they bowed head

31 And the people believed: and when they heard that the LORD had visited the children of Israel, and that he had looked upon their affliction, then they bowed their heads and worshipped.

Chapter 5

ספר שמות פרק ה
[שביעי]

וְאַחַ֗ר בָּ֚אוּ מֹשֶׁ֣ה וְאַהֲרֹ֔ן
and Aaron　Moses　they came　and afterward

וַיֹּאמְר֖וּ אֶל־פַּרְעֹ֑ה כֹּֽה־אָמַ֤ר יְהֹוָה֙ אֱלֹהֵ֣י יִשְׂרָאֵ֔ל
Israel　Elohim　ihvh　says - thus　Pharaoh - unto　and they said

שַׁלַּח אֶת־עַמִּי וְיָחֹגּוּ לִי בַּמִּדְבָּר׃
send that - my people and they festival to me in wilderness

1 And afterward Moses and Aaron went in, and told Pharaoh, Thus saith the LORD God of Israel, Let my people go, that they may hold a feast unto me in the wilderness.

וַיֹּאמֶר פַּרְעֹה
Pharaoh and he said

מִי יְהוָה אֲשֶׁר אֶשְׁמַע בְּקֹלוֹ לְשַׁלַּח אֶת־יִשְׂרָאֵל
who ihvh which I hear in his voice to send that - Israel

לֹא יָדַעְתִּי אֶת־יְהוָה
not I know that - ihvh

וְגַם אֶת־יִשְׂרָאֵל לֹא אֲשַׁלֵּחַ׃
and also that - Israel not I will send

2 And Pharaoh said, Who is the LORD, that I should obey his voice to let Israel go? I know not the LORD, neither will I let Israel go.

וַיֹּאמְרוּ אֱלֹהֵי הָעִבְרִים נִקְרָא עָלֵינוּ נֵלְכָה־נָּא דֶּרֶךְ
and they said Elohim the Hebrews met upon us now - we go way

שְׁלֹשֶׁת יָמִים בַּמִּדְבָּר
three days in wilderness

וְנִזְבְּחָה לַיהוָה אֱלֹהֵינוּ פֶּן־יִפְגָּעֵנוּ בַּדֶּבֶר אוֹ בֶחָרֶב׃
and we sacrifice to ihvh our Elohim lest - he strike us in pestilence or in sword

3 And they said, The God of the Hebrews hath met with us: let us go, we pray thee, three days' journey into the desert, and sacrifice unto the LORD our God; lest he fall upon us with pestilence, or with the sword.

וַיֹּאמֶר אֲלֵהֶם מֶלֶךְ מִצְרַיִם לָמָּה מֹשֶׁה וְאַהֲרֹן
and he said to them king Egypt why Moses and Aaron

תַּפְרִיעוּ אֶת־הָעָם מִמַּעֲשָׂיו
you turn it that - the people from it's work

לְכוּ לְסִבְלֹתֵיכֶם׃
you go to your burdens

4 And the king of Egypt said unto them, Wherefore do ye, Moses and Aaron, let the people from their works? get you unto your burdens.

וַיֹּאמֶר פַּרְעֹה הֵן־רַבִּים עַתָּה עַם־הָאָרֶץ
and he said Pharaoh them - numerous ones now the land - people

וְהִשְׁבַּתֶּם אֹתָם מִסִּבְלֹתָם׃
and you cause rest to them form their burdens

PARASHAT 1 CHAPTER 5

5 And Pharaoh said, Behold, the people of the land now are many, and ye make them rest from their burdens.

וַיְצַו פַּרְעֹה בַּיּוֹם הַהוּא אֶת־הַנֹּגְשִׂים בָּעָם
and he commanded Pharaoh in day the it the driver ones - that in people

וְאֶת־שֹׁטְרָיו לֵאמֹר׃
and that - his officers to say

6 And Pharaoh commanded the same day the taskmasters of the people, and their officers, saying,

לֹא תֹאסִפוּן לָתֵת תֶּבֶן לָעָם לִלְבֹּן הַלְּבֵנִים כִּתְמוֹל
not you continue to give straw to people to brick the bricks like yesterday

שִׁלְשֹׁם הֵם
before them

יֵלְכוּ וְקֹשְׁשׁוּ לָהֶם תֶּבֶן׃
they go and they bundle to them straw

7 Ye shall no more give the people straw to make brick, as heretofore: let them go and gather straw for themselves.

וְאֶת־מַתְכֹּנֶת הַלְּבֵנִים אֲשֶׁר הֵם עֹשִׂים תְּמוֹל שִׁלְשֹׁם
and that - quota the bricks which them making ones yesterday before

תָּשִׂימוּ עֲלֵיהֶם לֹא תִגְרְעוּ מִמֶּנּוּ
you put it upon them not you reduce it from him

כִּי־נִרְפִּים הֵם עַל־כֵּן הֵם צֹעֲקִים
like - idle ones them upon - thus them crying ones

לֵאמֹר נֵלְכָה נִזְבְּחָה לֵאלֹהֵינוּ׃
to say we go we sacrifice to our Elohim

8 And the tale of the bricks, which they did make heretofore, ye shall lay upon them; ye shall not diminish ought thereof: for they be idle; therefore they cry, saying, Let us go and sacrifice to our God.

תִּכְבַּד הָעֲבֹדָה עַל־הָאֲנָשִׁים
it be heavy the service upon - the men

וְיַעֲשׂוּ־בָהּ וְאַל־יִשְׁעוּ בְּדִבְרֵי־שָׁקֶר׃
and they do - in it and don't - they do in speakings - lie

9 Let there more work be laid upon the men, that they may labour therein; and let them not regard vain words.

וַיֵּצְאוּ נֹגְשֵׂי הָעָם וְשֹׁטְרָיו
and they went out driving ones the people and his officers

PARASHAT 1 CHAPTER 5

וַיֹּאמְרוּ אֶל־הָעָם לֵאמֹר כֹּה אָמַר פַּרְעֹה
Pharaoh   says   this   to say   the people - unto   and they said

אֵינֶנִּי נֹתֵן לָכֶם תֶּבֶן:
straw   to you   giver   not I

10 And the taskmasters of the people went out, and their officers, and they spake to the people, saying, Thus saith Pharaoh, I will not give you straw.

אַתֶּם לְכוּ קְחוּ לָכֶם תֶּבֶן מֵאֲשֶׁר תִּמְצָאוּ
you find it   from which   straw   to you   you take   you go   you

כִּי אֵין נִגְרָע מֵעֲבֹדַתְכֶם דָּבָר:
matter   from your service   diminished   isn't   like

11 Go ye, get you straw where ye can find it: yet not ought of your work shall be diminished.

וַיָּפֶץ הָעָם בְּכָל־אֶרֶץ מִצְרָיִם לְקֹשֵׁשׁ קַשׁ לַתֶּבֶן:
to straw   stubble   to bundle   Egypt   land - in all   the people   and he scattered

12 So the people were scattered abroad throughout all the land of Egypt to gather stubble instead of straw.

וְהַנֹּגְשִׂים אָצִים לֵאמֹר
to say   pressing ones   and the driver ones

כַּלּוּ מַעֲשֵׂיכֶם דְּבַר־יוֹם בְּיוֹמוֹ כַּאֲשֶׁר בִּהְיוֹת הַתֶּבֶן:
the straw   in there was   when   in it's day   day - matter   your tasks   you finish

13 And the taskmasters hasted them, saying, Fulfil your works, your daily tasks, as when there was straw.

וַיֻּכּוּ שֹׁטְרֵי בְּנֵי יִשְׂרָאֵל
Israel   sons   officers   and they struck

אֲשֶׁר־שָׂמוּ עֲלֵהֶם נֹגְשֵׂי פַרְעֹה לֵאמֹר
to say   Pharaoh   driver ones   upon them   they put - which

מַדּוּעַ לֹא כִלִּיתֶם חָקְכֶם לִלְבֹּן כִּתְמוֹל שִׁלְשֹׁם
before   like yesterday   to make brick   your take   you finished   not   why

גַּם־תְּמוֹל גַּם־הַיּוֹם:
the day - also   yesterday - also

14 And the officers of the children of Israel, which Pharaoh's taskmasters had set over them, were beaten, and demanded, Wherefore have ye not fulfilled your task in making brick both yesterday and today, as heretofore?

וַיָּבֹאוּ שֹׁטְרֵי בְּנֵי יִשְׂרָאֵל
Israel   sons   officers   and they came

וַיִּצְעֲקוּ אֶל־פַּרְעֹה לֵאמֹר
to say   Pharaoh - unto   and they cried

לָ֧מָּה תַעֲשֶׂ֛ה כֹ֖ה לַעֲבָדֶֽיךָ׃
to your servants　thus　you do　why

15 Then the officers of the children of Israel came and cried unto Pharaoh, saying, Wherefore dealest thou thus with thy servants?

תֶּ֚בֶן אֵ֣ין נִתָּ֣ן לַעֲבָדֶ֔יךָ
to your servants　given　isn't　straw

וּלְבֵנִ֛ים אֹמְרִ֥ים לָ֖נוּ עֲשׂ֑וּ
you make　to us　sayings　and bricks

וְהִנֵּ֧ה עֲבָדֶ֛יךָ מֻכִּ֖ים וְחָטָ֥את עַמֶּֽךָ׃
your people　and sin　beaten ones　your servants　and here

16 There is no straw given unto thy servants, and they say to us, Make brick: and, behold, thy servants are beaten; but the fault is in thine own people.

וַיֹּ֛אמֶר נִרְפִּ֥ים אַתֶּ֖ם נִרְפִּ֑ים
idle ones　you　idle ones　and he said

עַל־כֵּן֙ אַתֶּ֣ם אֹֽמְרִ֔ים נֵלְכָ֖ה נִזְבְּחָ֥ה לַיהוָֽה׃
to ihvh　we sacrifice　we go　sayings　you　thus - upon

17 But he said, Ye are idle, ye are idle: therefore ye say, Let us go and do sacrifice to the LORD.

וְעַתָּה֙ לְכ֣וּ עִבְד֔וּ וְתֶ֖בֶן לֹא־יִנָּתֵ֣ן לָכֶ֑ם
to you　it will be given - not　and straw　you serve　you go　and now

וְתֹ֥כֶן לְבֵנִ֖ים תִּתֵּֽנּוּ׃
you will give　bricks　and quota

18 Go therefore now, and work; for there shall no straw be given you, yet shall ye deliver the tale of bricks.

וַיִּרְא֞וּ שֹֽׁטְרֵ֧י בְנֵֽי־יִשְׂרָאֵ֛ל אֹתָ֖ם בְּרָ֣ע לֵאמֹ֑ר
to say　in bad　to them　Israel - sons　officers　and they saw

לֹא־תִגְרְע֥וּ מִלִּבְנֵיכֶ֖ם דְּבַר־י֥וֹם בְּיוֹמֽוֹ׃
in his day　day – matter　from your bricks　you reduce - not

19 And the officers of the children of Israel did see that they were in evil case, after it was said, Ye shall not minish ought from your bricks of your daily task.

וַֽיִּפְגְּעוּ֙ אֶת־מֹשֶׁ֣ה וְאֶֽת־אַהֲרֹ֔ן נִצָּבִ֖ים
standing ones　Aaron - and that　Moses - that　and they met

לִקְרָאתָ֑ם בְּצֵאתָ֖ם מֵאֵ֥ת פַּרְעֹֽה׃
Pharaoh　from that　in their going out　to meet them

20 And they met Moses and Aaron, who stood in the way, as they came forth from Pharaoh:

$$\text{וַיֹּאמְרוּ אֲלֵהֶם יֵרֶא יְהֹוָה עֲלֵיכֶם}$$
upon you   ihvh   he looks   unto them   and they said

$$\text{וְיִשְׁפֹּט אֲשֶׁר הִבְאַשְׁתֶּם אֶת־רֵיחֵנוּ בְּעֵינֵי פַרְעֹה}$$
Pharaoh   in eyes   our scent - that   cause you to stink   which   and he judge

$$\text{וּבְעֵינֵי עֲבָדָיו לָתֶת־חֶרֶב בְּיָדָם לְהָרְגֵנוּ:}$$
to kill us   in their hand   sword - to give   his servants   and in eyes

21 And they said unto them, The LORD look upon you, and judge; because ye have made our savour to be abhorred in the eyes of Pharaoh, and in the eyes of his servants, to put a sword in their hand to slay us.

[מפטיר]

$$\text{וַיָּשָׁב מֹשֶׁה אֶל־יְהֹוָה וַיֹּאמַר}$$
and he said   ihvh - unto   Moses   and he returned

$$\text{אֲדֹנָי לָמָה הֲרֵעֹתָה לָעָם הַזֶּה}$$
the this   to people   the you eviled   why   Adoni

$$\text{לָמָּה זֶּה שְׁלַחְתָּנִי:}$$
you sent me   this   why

22 And Moses returned unto the LORD, and said, Lord, wherefore hast thou so evil entreated this people? why is it that thou hast sent me?

$$\text{וּמֵאָז בָּאתִי אֶל־פַּרְעֹה לְדַבֵּר בִּשְׁמֶךָ הֵרַע לָעָם הַזֶּה}$$
the this   to people   the bad   in your name   to speak   Pharaoh - unto   I came   and from then

$$\text{וְהַצֵּל לֹא־הִצַּלְתָּ אֶת־עַמֶּךָ:}$$
your people – that   you rescued - not   and rescue

23 For since I came to Pharaoh to speak in thy name, he hath done evil to this people; neither hast thou delivered thy people at all.

CHAPTER 6

ספר שמות פרק ו

$$\text{וַיֹּאמֶר יְהֹוָה אֶל־מֹשֶׁה עַתָּה תִרְאֶה אֲשֶׁר אֶעֱשֶׂה לְפַרְעֹה}$$
to Pharaoh   I will do   which   you will see   now   Moses – unto   ihvh   and he said

$$\text{כִּי בְיָד חֲזָקָה יְשַׁלְּחֵם}$$
he will send them   mighty   in hand   like

$$\text{וּבְיָד חֲזָקָה יְגָרְשֵׁם מֵאַרְצוֹ:}$$
from his land   he will drive them   mighty   and in hand

1 Then the LORD said unto Moses, Now shalt thou see what I will do to Pharaoh: for with a strong hand shall he let them go, and with a strong hand shall he drive them out of his land.

ס ס ס

Parashat - Vaera

Chapter 6 cont

פרשת וארא

וַיְדַבֵּר אֱלֹהִים אֶל־מֹשֶׁה וַיֹּאמֶר אֵלָיו אֲנִי יְהוָה:
and he spoke   Elohim   Moses - unto   and he said   unto him   I   ihvh

2 And God spake unto Moses, and said unto him, I am the LORD:

וָאֵרָא אֶל־אַבְרָהָם אֶל־יִצְחָק וְאֶל־יַעֲקֹב בְּאֵל שַׁדָּי
and I appeared   Abraham - unto   and to Isaac - unto   Jacob – and unto   in El   Shadi

וּשְׁמִי יְהוָה לֹא נוֹדַעְתִּי לָהֶם:
and my name   ihvh   not   I made known   to them

3 And I appeared unto Abraham, unto Isaac, and unto Jacob, by the name of God Almighty, but by my name JEHOVAH was I not known to them.

וְגַם הֲקִמֹתִי אֶת־בְּרִיתִי אִתָּם לָתֵת לָהֶם
and also   I established   that - my covenant   with them   to give   to them

אֶת־אֶרֶץ כְּנָעַן אֵת אֶרֶץ מְגֻרֵיהֶם אֲשֶׁר־גָּרוּ בָהּ:
that - land   Canaan   that   land   their pilgrimage   which - they strangered   in it

4 And I have also established my covenant with them, to give them the land of Canaan, the land of their pilgrimage, wherein they were strangers.

וְגַם אֲנִי שָׁמַעְתִּי אֶת־נַאֲקַת בְּנֵי יִשְׂרָאֵל
and also   I   I heard   that - groaning   sons   Israel

אֲשֶׁר מִצְרַיִם מַעֲבִדִים אֹתָם
which   Egyptians   enslaving ones   to them

וָאֶזְכֹּר אֶת־בְּרִיתִי:
and I remembered   that - my covenant

5 And I have also heard the groaning of the children of Israel, whom the Egyptians keep in bondage; and I have remembered my covenant.

לָכֵן אֱמֹר לִבְנֵי־יִשְׂרָאֵל אֲנִי יְהוָה
to thus   say   Israel - to sons   I   ihvh

וְהוֹצֵאתִי אֶתְכֶם מִתַּחַת סִבְלֹת מִצְרַיִם
and I will bring out   that you   from under   burdens   Egyptians

וְהִצַּלְתִּי אֶתְכֶם מֵעֲבֹדָתָם וְגָאַלְתִּי אֶתְכֶם בִּזְרוֹעַ נְטוּיָה
and will rescue   that you   from their service   and I will redeem   that you   in arm   stretched

וּבִשְׁפָטִים גְּדֹלִים:
and in judgments   great ones

6 Wherefore say unto the children of Israel, I am the LORD, and I will bring you out from under the burdens of the Egyptians, and I will rid you out of their bondage, and I will redeem you with a stretched out arm, and with great judgments:

וְלָקַחְתִּ֨י אֶתְכֶ֥ם לִ֨י לְעָ֜ם
and I will to take   that them   to me   to people

וְהָיִ֤יתִי לָכֶם֙ לֵֽאלֹהִ֔ים וִֽידַעְתֶּ֗ם כִּ֣י אֲנִ֤י יְהוָה֙ אֱלֹ֣הֵיכֶ֔ם
and I will be   to you   to Elohim   I   like   and you will know   to Elohim   ihvh   your Elohim

הַמּוֹצִ֣יא אֶתְכֶ֔ם מִתַּ֖חַת סִבְל֥וֹת מִצְרָֽיִם׃
the bringer out   that you   from under   burdens   Egyptians

7 And I will take you to me for a people, and I will be to you a God: and ye shall know that I am the LORD your God, which bringeth you out from under the burdens of the Egyptians.

וְהֵבֵאתִ֤י אֶתְכֶם֙ אֶל־הָאָ֔רֶץ אֲשֶׁ֤ר נָשָׂ֨אתִי֙ אֶת־יָדִ֔י
and I will bring   that you   the land – unto   which   I swore   my hand – that

לָתֵ֣ת אֹתָ֔הּ לְאַבְרָהָ֥ם לְיִצְחָ֖ק וּֽלְיַעֲקֹ֑ב
to give   to it   to Abraham   to Isaac   and to Jacob

וְנָתַתִּ֨י אֹתָ֥הּ לָכֶ֛ם מוֹרָשָׁ֖ה אֲנִ֥י יְהוָֽה׃
and I will give   to it   to you   heritage   I   ihvh

8 And I will bring you in unto the land, concerning the which I did swear to give it to Abraham, to Isaac, and to Jacob; and I will give it you for an heritage: I am the LORD.

וַיְדַבֵּ֥ר מֹשֶׁ֛ה כֵּ֖ן אֶל־בְּנֵ֣י יִשְׂרָאֵ֑ל
and he spoke   Moshe   thus   sons – unto   Israel

וְלֹ֤א שָֽׁמְעוּ֙ אֶל־מֹשֶׁ֔ה מִקֹּ֣צֶר ר֔וּחַ וּמֵעֲבֹדָ֖ה קָשָֽׁה׃
and not   they heard   Moses – unto   from short   spirit   and from service   hard

9 And Moses spake so unto the children of Israel: but they hearkened not unto Moses for anguish of spirit, and for cruel bondage.

פ

וַיְדַבֵּ֥ר יְהוָ֖ה אֶל־מֹשֶׁ֥ה לֵּאמֹֽר׃
and he spoke   ihvh   Moses – unto   to say

10 And the LORD spake unto Moses, saying,

בֹּ֣א דַבֵּ֔ר אֶל־פַּרְעֹ֖ה מֶ֣לֶךְ מִצְרָ֑יִם
come   speak   Pharaoh – unto   king   Egyptians

וִֽישַׁלַּ֥ח אֶת־בְּנֵֽי־יִשְׂרָאֵ֖ל מֵאַרְצֽוֹ׃
and he send   Israel – sons – that   from his land

11 Go in, speak unto Pharaoh king of Egypt, that he let the children of Israel

50   PARASHAT 2   CHAPTER 6 CONT

go out of his land.

וַיְדַבֵּ֣ר מֹשֶׁ֔ה לִפְנֵ֥י יְהוָ֖ה לֵאמֹ֑ר
to say   ihvh   before   Moses   and he spoke

הֵ֤ן בְּנֵֽי־יִשְׂרָאֵל֙ לֹֽא־שָׁמְע֣וּ אֵלַ֔י
unto me   they heard – not   Israel – sons   thus

וְאֵיךְ֙ יִשְׁמָעֵ֣נִי פַרְעֹ֔ה וַאֲנִ֖י עֲרַ֥ל שְׂפָתָֽיִם׃
lips   uncircumcised   and I   Pharaoh   he hears me   and how

12 And Moses spake before the LORD, saying, Behold, the children of Israel have not hearkened unto me; how then shall Pharaoh hear me, who am of uncircumcised lips?

פ

וַיְדַבֵּ֤ר יְהוָה֙ אֶל־מֹשֶׁ֣ה וְאֶֽל־אַהֲרֹ֔ן
Aaron – and unto   Moses – unto   ihvh   and he spoke

וַיְצַוֵּם֙ אֶל־בְּנֵ֣י יִשְׂרָאֵ֔ל וְאֶל־פַּרְעֹ֖ה מֶ֣לֶךְ מִצְרָ֑יִם
Egyptians   king   Pharaoh – and unto   Israel   sons – unto   and he commanded them

לְהוֹצִ֥יא אֶת־בְּנֵֽי־יִשְׂרָאֵ֖ל מֵאֶ֥רֶץ מִצְרָֽיִם׃
Egypt   from land   Israel – sons – that   to bring out

13 And the LORD spake unto Moses and unto Aaron, and gave them a charge unto the children of Israel, and unto Pharaoh king of Egypt, to bring the children of Israel out of the land of Egypt.

ס

[שני]

אֵ֖לֶּה רָאשֵׁ֣י בֵית־אֲבֹתָ֑ם בְּנֵ֨י
sons   their fathers - house   heads   these

רְאוּבֵ֜ן בְּכֹ֣ר יִשְׂרָאֵ֗ל
Israel   first born   Reuben

חֲנ֤וֹךְ וּפַלּוּא֙ חֶצְרֹ֣ן וְכַרְמִ֔י אֵ֖לֶּה מִשְׁפְּחֹ֥ת רְאוּבֵֽן׃
Reuben   families   these   and Carmi   Hezron   and Pallu   Hanoch

14 These be the heads of their fathers' houses: The sons of Reuben the firstborn of Israel; Hanoch, and Pallu, Hezron, and Carmi: these be the families of Reuben.

וּבְנֵ֣י שִׁמְע֗וֹן יְמוּאֵ֨ל וְיָמִ֤ין וְאֹ֙הַד֙ וְיָכִ֣ין וְצֹ֔חַר וְשָׁא֖וּל
and Shaul   and Zohar   and Jachin   and Ohad   and Jamin   Jemuel   Simeon   and sons

בֶּן־הַֽכְּנַעֲנִ֑ית אֵ֖לֶּה מִשְׁפְּחֹ֥ת שִׁמְעֽוֹן׃
Simeon   families   these   Canaanitish woman – son

15 And the sons of Simeon; Jemuel, and Jamin, and Ohad, and Jachin, and

Zohar, and Shaul the son of a Canaanitish woman: these are the families of Simeon.

וְאֵלֶּה שְׁמוֹת בְּנֵי־לֵוִי לְתֹלְדֹתָם
and these names Levi – sons to their generations

גֵּרְשׁוֹן וּקְהָת וּמְרָרִי
Gershon and Kohath and Merari

וּשְׁנֵי חַיֵּי לֵוִי שֶׁבַע וּשְׁלֹשִׁים וּמְאַת שָׁנָה׃
and years life Levi seven and thirty and hundred year

16 And these are the names of the sons of Levi according to their generations; Gershon, and Kohath, and Merari: and the years of the life of Levi were an hundred thirty and seven years.

בְּנֵי גֵרְשׁוֹן לִבְנִי וְשִׁמְעִי לְמִשְׁפְּחֹתָם׃
sons Gershon Libni and Shimi to their families

17 The sons of Gershon; Libni, and Shimi, according to their families.

וּבְנֵי קְהָת עַמְרָם וְיִצְהָר וְחֶבְרוֹן וְעֻזִּיאֵל
and sons Kohath Amram and Izhar and Hebron and Uzziel

וּשְׁנֵי חַיֵּי קְהָת שָׁלֹשׁ וּשְׁלֹשִׁים וּמְאַת שָׁנָה׃
and years life Kohath three and thirty and hundred year

18 And the sons of Kohath; Amram, and Izhar, and Hebron, and Uzziel: and the years of the life of Kohath were an hundred thirty and three years.

וּבְנֵי מְרָרִי מַחְלִי וּמוּשִׁי
and sons Merari Mahali and Mushi

אֵלֶּה מִשְׁפְּחֹת הַלֵּוִי לְתֹלְדֹתָם׃
these families the Levi to generations

19 And the sons of Merari; Mahali and Mushi: these are the families of Levi according to their generations.

וַיִּקַּח עַמְרָם אֶת־יוֹכֶבֶד דֹּדָתוֹ לוֹ לְאִשָּׁה
and he took Amram Jochebed – that his aunt to him to wife

וַתֵּלֶד לוֹ אֶת־אַהֲרֹן וְאֶת־מֹשֶׁה
and she bore to him Aaron – that Moses – and that

וּשְׁנֵי חַיֵּי עַמְרָם שֶׁבַע וּשְׁלֹשִׁים וּמְאַת שָׁנָה׃
and years life Amram seven and thirty and hundred year

20 And Amram took him Jochebed his father's sister to wife; and she bare him Aaron and Moses: and the years of the life of Amram were an hundred and thirty and seven years.

וּבְנֵי יִצְהָר קֹרַח וָנֶפֶג וְזִכְרִי׃
and sons Izhar Korah and Nepheg and Zichri

21 And the sons of Izhar; Korah, and Nepheg, and Zichri.

וּבְנֵי עֻזִּיאֵל מִישָׁאֵל וְאֶלְצָפָן וְסִתְרִי:
and sons　Uzziel　Mishael　and Elzaphan　and Zithri

22 And the sons of Uzziel; Mishael, and Elzaphan, and Zithri.

וַיִּקַּח אַהֲרֹן אֶת־אֱלִישֶׁבַע
and he took　Aaron　that – Elisheba

בַּת־עַמִּינָדָב אֲחוֹת נַחְשׁוֹן לוֹ לְאִשָּׁה
Amminadab – daughter　sister　Naashon　to him　to wife

וַתֵּלֶד לוֹ
and she bare　to him

אֶת־נָדָב וְאֶת־אֲבִיהוּא אֶת־אֶלְעָזָר וְאֶת־אִיתָמָר:
Nadab – that　Abihu – and that　Eleazar – and that　Ithamar – and that

23 And Aaron took him Elisheba, daughter of Amminadab, sister of Naashon, to wife; and she bare him Nadab, and Abihu, Eleazar, and Ithamar.

וּבְנֵי קֹרַח אַסִּיר וְאֶלְקָנָה וַאֲבִיאָסָף
and sons　Korah　Assir　and Elkanah　and Abiasaph

אֵלֶּה מִשְׁפְּחֹת הַקָּרְחִי:
these　families　the Korhites

24 And the sons of Korah; Assir, and Elkanah, and Abiasaph: these are the families of the Korhites.

וְאֶלְעָזָר בֶּן־אַהֲרֹן לָקַח־לוֹ מִבְּנוֹת פּוּטִיאֵל לוֹ לְאִשָּׁה
and Eleazar　Aaron – son　to him – took　from daughters　Putiel　to him　to wife

וַתֵּלֶד לוֹ אֶת־פִּינְחָס
and she bare　to him　that – Phinehas

אֵלֶּה רָאשֵׁי אֲבוֹת הַלְוִיִּם לְמִשְׁפְּחֹתָם:
these　heads　fathers　the Levi　to their families

25 And Eleazar Aaron's son took him one of the daughters of Putiel to wife; and she bare him Phinehas: these are the heads of the fathers of the Levites according to their families.

הוּא אַהֲרֹן וּמֹשֶׁה אֲשֶׁר אָמַר יְהוָה לָהֶם
he　Aaron　and Moses　which　said　ihvh　to them

הוֹצִיאוּ אֶת־בְּנֵי יִשְׂרָאֵל מֵאֶרֶץ מִצְרַיִם עַל־צִבְאֹתָם:
you bring out　that – sons　Israel　from land　Egyptian　upon – their armies

26 These are that Aaron and Moses, to whom the LORD said, Bring out the children of Israel from the land of Egypt according to their armies.

PARASHAT 2　CHAPTER 6 CONT　53

הֵם הַמְדַבְּרִים אֶל־פַּרְעֹה מֶלֶךְ־מִצְרַיִם
Egyptians – king   Pharaoh – unto   the speakings   them

לְהוֹצִיא אֶת־בְּנֵי־יִשְׂרָאֵל מִמִּצְרָיִם הוּא מֹשֶׁה וְאַהֲרֹן׃
and Aaron   Moses   he   from Egypt   Israel – sons – that   to bring out

27 These are they which spake to Pharaoh king of Egypt, to bring out the children of Israel from Egypt: these are that Moses and Aaron.

וַיְהִי בְּיוֹם דִּבֶּר יְהֹוָה אֶל־מֹשֶׁה בְּאֶרֶץ מִצְרָיִם׃
Egypt   in land   Moses – unto   ihvh   he spoke   in day   and it was

28 And it came to pass on the day when the LORD spake unto Moses in the land of Egypt,

ס

[שלישי]

וַיְדַבֵּר יְהֹוָה אֶל־מֹשֶׁה לֵּאמֹר אֲנִי יְהֹוָה
ihvh   I   to say   Moses – unto   ihvh   and he spoke

דַּבֵּר אֶל־פַּרְעֹה מֶלֶךְ מִצְרַיִם אֵת כָּל־אֲשֶׁר אֲנִי דֹּבֵר אֵלֶיךָ׃
unto you   speak   I   which – all   that   Egypt   king   Pharaoh – unto   speak

29 That the LORD spake unto Moses, saying, I am the LORD: speak thou unto Pharaoh king of Egypt all that I say unto thee.

וַיֹּאמֶר מֹשֶׁה לִפְנֵי יְהֹוָה הֵן אֲנִי עֲרַל שְׂפָתַיִם
lips   uncircumcised   I   thus   ihvh   before   Moses   and he said

וְאֵיךְ יִשְׁמַע אֵלַי פַּרְעֹה׃
Pharaoh   unto me   he will hear   and how

30 And Moses said before the LORD, Behold, I am of uncircumcised lips, and how shall Pharaoh hearken unto me?

פ

Chapter 7

ספר שמות פרק ז

וַיֹּאמֶר יְהֹוָה אֶל־מֹשֶׁה רְאֵה נְתַתִּיךָ אֱלֹהִים לְפַרְעֹה
to Pharaoh   Elohim   I give you   see   Moses – unto   ihvh   and he said

וְאַהֲרֹן אָחִיךָ יִהְיֶה נְבִיאֶךָ׃
your prophet   he will be   your brother   and Aaron

1 And the LORD said unto Moses, See, I have made thee a god to Pharaoh: and Aaron thy brother shall be thy prophet.

אַתָּה תְדַבֵּר אֵת כָּל־אֲשֶׁר אֲצַוֶּךָּ
I command you   which – all   that   you will speak   you

וְאַהֲרֹן אָחִיךָ יְדַבֵּר אֶל־פַּרְעֹה
Pharaoh – unto   he will speak   your brother   and Aaron

וְשִׁלַּח אֶת־בְּנֵי־יִשְׂרָאֵל מֵאַרְצוֹ:
from his land   Israel – sons – that   and send

2 Thou shalt speak all that I command thee: and Aaron thy brother shall speak unto Pharaoh, that he send the children of Israel out of his land.

וַאֲנִי אַקְשֶׁה אֶת־לֵב פַּרְעֹה וְהִרְבֵּיתִי אֶת־אֹתֹתַי
my signs – that   and cause to multiply   Pharaoh   heart – that   I will harden   and I

וְאֶת־מוֹפְתַי בְּאֶרֶץ מִצְרָיִם:
Egypt   in land   my wonders – and that

3 And I will harden Pharaoh's heart, and multiply my signs and my wonders in the land of Egypt.

וְלֹא־יִשְׁמַע אֲלֵכֶם פַּרְעֹה וְנָתַתִּי אֶת־יָדִי בְּמִצְרָיִם
in Egypt   my hand – that   and will I give   Pharaoh   unto you   he will hear – and not

וְהוֹצֵאתִי אֶת־צִבְאֹתַי אֶת־עַמִּי בְנֵי־יִשְׂרָאֵל
Israel – sons   my people – that   my armies – that   and I will bring out

מֵאֶרֶץ מִצְרַיִם בִּשְׁפָטִים גְּדֹלִים:
big ones   in judgments   Egypt   from land

4 But Pharaoh shall not hearken unto you, that I may lay my hand upon Egypt, and bring forth mine armies, and my people the children of Israel, out of the land of Egypt by great judgments.

וְיָדְעוּ מִצְרַיִם כִּי־אֲנִי יְהוָה בִּנְטֹתִי אֶת־יָדִי עַל־מִצְרָיִם
Egypt – upon   my hand – that   in I stretch   ihvh   I – like   Egypt   and they know

וְהוֹצֵאתִי אֶת־בְּנֵי־יִשְׂרָאֵל מִתּוֹכָם:
from their midst   Israel – sons – that   and I bring out

5 And the Egyptians shall know that I am the LORD, when I stretch forth mine hand upon Egypt, and bring out the children of Israel from among them.

וַיַּעַשׂ מֹשֶׁה וְאַהֲרֹן כַּאֲשֶׁר צִוָּה יְהוָה אֹתָם כֵּן עָשׂוּ:
they did thus   to them   ihvh   commanded   when   and Aaron   Moses   and did

6 And Moses and Aaron did as the LORD commanded them, so did they.

וּמֹשֶׁה בֶּן־שְׁמֹנִים שָׁנָה
years   eighty – age   and Moses

וְאַהֲרֹן בֶּן־שָׁלֹשׁ וּשְׁמֹנִים שָׁנָה בְּדַבְּרָם אֶל־פַּרְעֹה:
Pharaoh – unto   in their speaking   years   and eighty   three – age   and Aaron

7 And Moses was fourscore years old, and Aaron fourscore and three years old, when they spake unto Pharaoh.

PARASHAT 2   CHAPTER 7

פ

[רביעי]

וַיֹּאמֶר יְהוָה אֶל־מֹשֶׁה וְאֶל־אַהֲרֹן לֵאמֹר׃
_{to say   Aaron – and unto   Moses – unto   ihvh   and he said}

8 And the LORD spake unto Moses and unto Aaron, saying,

כִּי יְדַבֵּר אֲלֵכֶם פַּרְעֹה לֵאמֹר תְּנוּ לָכֶם מוֹפֵת
_{miracle to you you give to say Pharaoh unto you he will speak like}

וְאָמַרְתָּ אֶל־אַהֲרֹן קַח אֶת־מַטְּךָ
_{your rod – that take Aaron – unto and you say}

וְהַשְׁלֵךְ לִפְנֵי־פַרְעֹה יְהִי לְתַנִּין׃
_{to serpent it will be Pharaoh – before and the throw}

9 When Pharaoh shall speak unto you, saying, Shew a miracle for you: then thou shalt say unto Aaron, Take thy rod, and cast it before Pharaoh, and it shall become a serpent.

וַיָּבֹא מֹשֶׁה וְאַהֲרֹן אֶל־פַּרְעֹה
_{Pharaoh – unto and Aaron Moses and he came}

וַיַּעֲשׂוּ־כֵן כַּאֲשֶׁר צִוָּה יְהוָה
_{ihvh commanded when thus – and he did}

וַיַּשְׁלֵךְ אַהֲרֹן אֶת־מַטֵּהוּ לִפְנֵי פַרְעֹה
_{Pharaoh before his rod – that Aaron and they threw}

וְלִפְנֵי עֲבָדָיו וַיְהִי לְתַנִּין׃
_{to serpent and it was his servants and before}

10 And Moses and Aaron went in unto Pharaoh, and they did so as the LORD had commanded: and Aaron cast down his rod before Pharaoh, and before his servants, and it became a serpent.

וַיִּקְרָא גַּם־פַּרְעֹה לַחֲכָמִים וְלַמְכַשְּׁפִים
_{and to sorcerers to wise ones Pharaoh – also and he called}

וַיַּעֲשׂוּ גַם־הֵם חַרְטֻמֵּי מִצְרַיִם בְּלַהֲטֵיהֶם כֵּן׃
_{thus in their enchantments Egypt magicians them - also and they did}

11 Then Pharaoh also called the wise men and the sorcerers: now the magicians of Egypt, they also did in like manner with their enchantments.

וַיַּשְׁלִיכוּ אִישׁ מַטֵּהוּ וַיִּהְיוּ לְתַנִּינִם
_{to serpents and they were his rod man and they cast down}

וַיִּבְלַע מַטֵּה־אַהֲרֹן אֶת־מַטֹּתָם׃
_{their rods – that Aaron – rod and it swallowed}

12 For they cast down every man his rod, and they became serpents: but Aaron's rod swallowed up their rods.

וַיֶּחֱזַק֙ לֵ֣ב פַּרְעֹ֔ה
and he hardened heart Pharaoh

וְלֹ֥א שָׁמַ֖ע אֲלֵהֶ֑ם כַּאֲשֶׁ֖ר דִּבֶּ֥ר יְהוָֽה׃
and not hear unto them when spoke ihvh

13 And he hardened Pharaoh's heart, that he hearkened not unto them; as the LORD had said.

ס

וַיֹּ֤אמֶר יְהוָה֙ אֶל־מֹשֶׁ֔ה כָּבֵ֖ד לֵ֣ב פַּרְעֹ֑ה מֵאֵ֖ן לְשַׁלַּ֥ח הָעָֽם׃
and he said ihvh Moses – unto heavy heart Pharaoh refusing to send the people

14 And the LORD said unto Moses, Pharaoh's heart is hardened, he refuseth to let the people go.

לֵ֣ךְ אֶל־פַּרְעֹ֞ה בַּבֹּ֗קֶר הִנֵּה֙ יֹצֵ֣א הַמַּ֔יְמָה
go Pharaoh – unto in morning here he comes out the towards water

וְנִצַּבְתָּ֥ לִקְרָאת֖וֹ עַל־שְׂפַ֣ת הַיְאֹ֑ר
and you stand to his meet upon – beach the river

וְהַמַּטֶּ֛ה אֲשֶׁר־נֶהְפַּ֥ךְ לְנָחָ֖שׁ תִּקַּ֥ח בְּיָדֶֽךָ׃
and the rod which – transformed to serpent you will take in your hand

15 Get thee unto Pharaoh in the morning; lo, he goeth out unto the water; and thou shalt stand by the river's brink against he come; and the rod which was turned to a serpent shalt thou take in thine hand.

וְאָמַרְתָּ֣ אֵלָ֗יו יְהוָ֞ה אֱלֹהֵ֤י הָעִבְרִים֙ שְׁלָחַ֣נִי אֵלֶ֣יךָ לֵאמֹ֔ר
and you will say unto him ihvh Elohim the Hebrews sent me unto you to say

שַׁלַּח֙ אֶת־עַמִּ֔י וְיַֽעַבְדֻ֖נִי בַּמִּדְבָּ֑ר
send that – my people and they serve me in wilderness

וְהִנֵּ֥ה לֹא־שָׁמַ֖עְתָּ עַד־כֹּֽה׃
and here not – you hear till – thus

16 And thou shalt say unto him, The LORD God of the Hebrews hath sent me unto thee, saying, Let my people go, that they may serve me in the wilderness: and, behold, hitherto thou wouldest not hear.

כֹּ֚ה אָמַ֣ר יְהוָ֔ה בְּזֹ֣את תֵּדַ֔ע
thus say ihvh in this you know

כִּ֖י אֲנִ֣י יְהוָ֑ה הִנֵּ֨ה אָנֹכִ֜י מַכֶּ֣ה בַּמַּטֶּ֣ה
like I ihvh here I am strike in rod

אֲשֶׁר־בְּיָדִ֗י עַל־הַמַּ֛יִם אֲשֶׁ֥ר בַּיְאֹ֖ר
which – in my hand upon – the water which in river

PARASHAT 2   CHAPTER 7

וְנֶהֶפְכ֖וּ	לְדָֽם׃
and cause it to turn	to blood

17 Thus saith the LORD, In this thou shalt know that I am the LORD: behold, I will smite with the rod that is in mine hand upon the waters which are in the river, and they shall be turned to blood.

וְהַדָּגָ֧ה	אֲשֶׁר־בַּיְאֹ֛ר	תָּמ֖וּת	וּבָאַ֣שׁ	הַיְאֹ֑ר
and the fish	in river – which	it will die	and stink	the river

וְנִלְא֣וּ	מִצְרַ֔יִם	לִשְׁתּ֥וֹת	מַ֖יִם	מִן־הַיְאֹֽר׃
and they will loathe	Egyptians	to drink	water	the river – from

18 And the fish that is in the river shall die, and the river shall stink; and the Egyptians shall loathe to drink of the water of the river.

ס

וַיֹּ֨אמֶר יְהוָ֜ה אֶל־מֹשֶׁ֗ה אֱמֹ֣ר אֶֽל־אַהֲרֹ֡ן קַ֣ח מַטְּךָ֣
and he said ihvh unto – Moses say unto – Aaron take your rod

וּנְטֵֽה־יָדְךָ֣	עַל־מֵימֵ֣י	מִצְרַ֡יִם	עַֽל־נַהֲרֹתָ֣ם ׀	עַל־יְאֹרֵיהֶם֩
and stretch out – your hand	waters – upon	Egypt	their streams – upon	their rivers – upon

וְעַל־אַגְמֵיהֶ֨ם	וְעַ֜ל	כָּל־מִקְוֵ֧ה	מֵימֵיהֶ֛ם
and upon – their ponds	and upon	baths – all	their waters

וְיִֽהְיוּ־דָ֑ם	וְהָ֤יָה	דָם֙	בְּכָל־אֶ֣רֶץ מִצְרַ֔יִם
blood – and they be	and it will be	blood	land – in all Egypt

וּבָעֵצִ֖ים	וּבָאֲבָנִֽים׃
and in woods	and in stones

19 And the LORD spake unto Moses, Say unto Aaron, Take thy rod, and stretch out thine hand upon the waters of Egypt, upon their streams, upon their rivers, and upon their ponds, and upon all their pools of water, that they may become blood; and that there may be blood throughout all the land of Egypt, both in vessels of wood, and in vessels of stone.

וַיַּֽעֲשׂוּ־כֵן֩	מֹשֶׁ֨ה וְאַהֲרֹ֜ן	כַּאֲשֶׁ֣ר ׀ צִוָּ֣ה	יְהוָ֗ה
thus – and they did	Moses and Aaron	when commanded	ihvh

וַיָּ֤רֶם	בַּמַּטֶּה֙	וַיַּ֣ךְ	אֶת־הַמַּ֣יִם	אֲשֶׁ֣ר בַּיְאֹ֗ר	לְעֵינֵ֥י פַרְעֹ֛ה
and he lifted	in rod	and he smote	the water _ that	which in river	to eye Pharaoh

וּלְעֵינֵ֣י עֲבָדָ֑יו	וַיֵּהָֽפְכ֛וּ	כָּל־הַמַּ֥יִם	אֲשֶׁר־בַּיְאֹ֖ר	לְדָֽם׃
and to eyes his servants	and they turned	like waters – all	in river – which	to blood

20 And Moses and Aaron did so, as the LORD commanded; and he lifted up the rod, and smote the waters that were in the river, in the sight of Pharaoh, and in the sight of his servants; and all the waters that were in the river were turned to blood.

וְהַדָּגָה אֲשֶׁר־בַּיְאֹר מֵתָה וַיִּבְאַשׁ הַיְאֹר
the river   and it stank   died   in river – which   and the fish

וְלֹא־יָכְלוּ מִצְרַיִם לִשְׁתּוֹת מַיִם מִן־הַיְאֹר
the river – from   water   to drink   Egyptians   they able – and not

וַיְהִי הַדָּם בְּכָל־אֶרֶץ מִצְרָיִם׃
Egypt   land – in all   the blood   and it was

21 And the fish that was in the river died; and the river stank, and the Egyptians could not drink of the water of the river; and there was blood throughout all the land of Egypt.

וַיַּעֲשׂוּ־כֵן חַרְטֻמֵּי מִצְרַיִם בְּלָטֵיהֶם
in their enchantments   Egypt   magicians   thus – and they did

וַיֶּחֱזַק לֵב־פַּרְעֹה
Pharaoh – heart   and he hardened

וְלֹא־שָׁמַע אֲלֵהֶם כַּאֲשֶׁר דִּבֶּר יְהוָה׃
ihvh   spoke   when   unto them   hear – and not

22 And the magicians of Egypt did so with their enchantments: and Pharaoh's heart was hardened, neither did he hearken unto them; as the LORD had said.

וַיִּפֶן פַּרְעֹה וַיָּבֹא אֶל־בֵּיתוֹ
his house – unto   and he came   Pharaoh   and he turned

וְלֹא־שָׁת לִבּוֹ גַּם־לָזֹאת׃
to this – also   his heart   set – and not

23 And Pharaoh turned and went into his house, neither did he set his heart to this also.

וַיַּחְפְּרוּ כָל־מִצְרַיִם סְבִיבֹת הַיְאֹר מַיִם לִשְׁתּוֹת
to drink   water   the river   round   Egyptians – all   and they dug

כִּי לֹא יָכְלוּ לִשְׁתֹּת מִמֵּימֵי הַיְאֹר׃
the river   from waters   to drink   they able   not   like

24 And all the Egyptians digged round about the river for water to drink; for they could not drink of the water of the river.

וַיִּמָּלֵא שִׁבְעַת יָמִים אַחֲרֵי הַכּוֹת־יְהוָה אֶת־הַיְאֹר׃
the river – that   ihvh – smitten   after   days   seven   and it filled

25 And seven days were fulfilled, after that the LORD had smitten the river.

פ

Chapter 8

ספר שמות פרק ח

וַיֹּאמֶר יְהוָה אֶל־מֹשֶׁה בֹּא אֶל־פַּרְעֹה וְאָמַרְתָּ אֵלָיו
and he said ihvh Moses – unto come Pharaoh – unto and you say unto him

כֹּה אָמַר יְהוָה שַׁלַּח אֶת־עַמִּי וְיַעַבְדֻנִי:
thus says ihvh send my people – that and they will serve me

1 And the LORD spake unto Moses, Go unto Pharaoh, and say unto him, Thus saith the LORD, Let my people go, that they may serve me.

וְאִם־מָאֵן אַתָּה לְשַׁלֵּחַ
refuse – and if you to send

הִנֵּה אָנֹכִי נֹגֵף אֶת־כָּל־גְּבוּלְךָ בַּצְפַרְדְּעִים:
here I am strike that – all – your borders in frogs

2 And if thou refuse to let them go, behold, I will smite all thy borders with frogs:

וְשָׁרַץ הַיְאֹר צְפַרְדְּעִים
and will creep the river frogs

וְעָלוּ וּבָאוּ בְּבֵיתֶךָ
and they will ascend and they will come in your house

וּבַחֲדַר מִשְׁכָּבְךָ וְעַל־מִטָּתֶךָ
and in room your bedchamber and upon - your bed

וּבְבֵית עֲבָדֶיךָ וּבְעַמֶּךָ
and in house your servant and in your people

וּבְתַנּוּרֶיךָ וּבְמִשְׁאֲרוֹתֶיךָ:
and in your ovens and in your kneading troughs

3 And the river shall bring forth frogs abundantly, which shall go up and come into thine house, and into thy bedchamber, and upon thy bed, and into the house of thy servants, and upon thy people, and into thine ovens, and into thy kneading troughs:

וּבְכָה וּבְעַמְּךָ וּבְכָל־עֲבָדֶיךָ
and in thus and in your people and in all – your servants

יַעֲלוּ הַצְפַרְדְּעִים:
they will ascend the frogs

4 And the frogs shall come up both on thee, and upon thy people, and upon all thy servants.

וַיֹּאמֶר יְהוָה אֶל־מֹשֶׁה אֱמֹר אֶל־אַהֲרֹן
and he said ihvh Moses – unto say Aaron – unto

נְטֵה אֶת־יָדְךָ בְּמַטֶּךָ עַל־הַנְּהָרֹת עַל־הַיְאֹרִים וְעַל־הָאֲגַמִּים
the ponds – and upon · the rivers – upon · the streams – upon · in your rod · your hand – that stretch

וְהַעַל אֶת־הַצְפַרְדְּעִים עַל־אֶרֶץ מִצְרָיִם:
Egypt · land – upon · the frogs – that · and the ascend

5 And the LORD spake unto Moses, Say unto Aaron, Stretch forth thine hand with thy rod over the streams, over the rivers, and over the ponds, and cause frogs to come up upon the land of Egypt.

וַיֵּט אַהֲרֹן אֶת־יָדוֹ עַל מֵימֵי מִצְרָיִם
Egypt · waters · upon · his hand – that · Aaron · and he stretched

וַתַּעַל הַצְּפַרְדֵּעַ וַתְּכַס אֶת־אֶרֶץ מִצְרָיִם:
Egypt · land – that · and it covered · the frog · and it ascended

6 And Aaron stretched out his hand over the waters of Egypt; and the frogs came up, and covered the land of Egypt.

וַיַּעֲשׂוּ־כֵן הַחַרְטֻמִּים בְּלָטֵיהֶם
in their enchantments · the magicians · thus – and he did

וַיַּעֲלוּ אֶת־הַצְפַרְדְּעִים עַל־אֶרֶץ מִצְרָיִם:
Egypt · land – upon · the frogs – that · and they ascended

7 And the magicians did so with their enchantments, and brought up frogs upon the land of Egypt.

וַיִּקְרָא פַרְעֹה לְמֹשֶׁה וּלְאַהֲרֹן וַיֹּאמֶר
and he said · and to Aaron · to Moses · Pharaoh · and he called

הַעְתִּירוּ אֶל־יְהֹוָה מִמֶּנִּי וּמֵעַמִּי
and from my people · from me · ihvh – unto · the you entreat

וְיָסֵר הַצְפַרְדְּעִים וַאֲשַׁלְּחָה אֶת־הָעָם וְיִזְבְּחוּ לַיהֹוָה:
to ihvh · and they sacrifice · the people – that · and I will send · the frogs · and he remove

8 Then Pharaoh called for Moses and Aaron, and said, Entreat the LORD, that he may take away the frogs from me, and from my people; and I will let the people go, that they may do sacrifice unto the LORD.

וַיֹּאמֶר מֹשֶׁה לְפַרְעֹה הִתְפָּאֵר עָלַי
upon me · cause to vaunt · to Pharaoh · Moses · and he said

לְמָתַי אַעְתִּיר לְךָ וְלַעֲבָדֶיךָ וּלְעַמְּךָ
and to your people · and to your servants · to you · I will entreat · to when

לְהַכְרִית הַצְפַרְדְּעִים מִמְּךָ וּמִבָּתֶּיךָ רַק בַּיְאֹר תִּשָּׁאַרְנָה:
it will remain · in river · only · and from your houses · from you · the frogs · to the destroy

9 And Moses said unto Pharaoh, Glory over me: when shall I entreat for thee, and for thy servants, and for thy people, to destroy the frogs from thee and thy houses, that they may remain in the river only?

וַיֹּאמֶר לְמָחָר
and he said   to tomorrow

וַיֹּאמֶר כִּדְבָרְךָ לְמַעַן תֵּדַע כִּי־אֵין כַּיהוָה אֱלֹהֵינוּ׃
and he said   like you said   to end   you will know   isn't–like   like ihvh   our Elolim

10 And he said, Tomorrow. And he said, Be it according to thy word: that thou mayest know that there is none like unto the LORD our God.

[חמישי]

וְסָרוּ הַצְפַרְדְּעִים מִמְּךָ
and they will depart   the frogs   from you

וּמִבָּתֶּיךָ וּמֵעֲבָדֶיךָ וּמֵעַמֶּךָ
and from your house   and from your servant   and from your people

רַק בַּיְאֹר תִּשָּׁאַרְנָה׃
only   in river   it will remain

11 And the frogs shall depart from thee, and from thy houses, and from thy servants, and from thy people; they shall remain in the river only.

וַיֵּצֵא מֹשֶׁה וְאַהֲרֹן מֵעִם פַּרְעֹה
and he came out   Moses   and Aaron   from with   Pharaoh

וַיִּצְעַק מֹשֶׁה אֶל־יְהוָה
and he cried   Moses   ihvh–unto

עַל־דְּבַר הַצְפַרְדְּעִים אֲשֶׁר־שָׂם לְפַרְעֹה׃
matter–upon   the frogs   put–which   to Pharaoh

12 And Moses and Aaron went out from Pharaoh: and Moses cried unto the LORD because of the frogs which he had brought against Pharaoh.

וַיַּעַשׂ יְהוָה כִּדְבַר מֹשֶׁה
and he did   ihvh   like spoke   Moses

וַיָּמֻתוּ הַצְפַרְדְּעִים מִן־הַבָּתִּים מִן־הַחֲצֵרֹת וּמִן־הַשָּׂדֹת׃
and they died   the frogs   the houses–from   the courts–from   the fields–and from

13 And the LORD did according to the word of Moses; and the frogs died out of the houses, out of the villages, and out of the fields.

וַיִּצְבְּרוּ אֹתָם חֳמָרִם חֳמָרִם וַתִּבְאַשׁ הָאָרֶץ׃
and they piled   to them   heaps   heaps   and it stank   the land

14 And they gathered them together upon heaps: and the land stank.

וַיַּרְא פַּרְעֹה כִּי הָיְתָה הָרְוָחָה
and he saw   Pharaoh   like   it was   the respite

וְהַכְבֵּד אֶת־לִבּוֹ
and the heavy   his heart–that

וְלֹא שָׁמַע אֲלֵהֶם כַּאֲשֶׁר דִּבֶּר יְהוָה:
ihvh   spoke   when   unto them   heard   and not

15 But when Pharaoh saw that there was respite, he hardened his heart, and hearkened not unto them; as the LORD had said.

ס

וַיֹּאמֶר יְהוָה אֶל־מֹשֶׁה אֱמֹר אֶל־אַהֲרֹן נְטֵה אֶת־מַטְּךָ
your rod – that   stretch   Aaron – unto   say   Moses – unto   ihvh   and he said

וְהַךְ אֶת־עֲפַר הָאָרֶץ
the land   dust – that   and smite

וְהָיָה לְכִנִּם בְּכָל־אֶרֶץ מִצְרָיִם:
Egypt   land – in all   to lice   and it will be

16 And the LORD said unto Moses, Say unto Aaron, Stretch out thy rod, and smite the dust of the land, that it may become lice throughout all the land of Egypt.

וַיַּעֲשׂוּ־כֵן וַיֵּט אַהֲרֹן אֶת־יָדוֹ בְמַטֵּהוּ
in his rod   his hand – that   Aaron   and he stretched   thus – and they did

וַיַּךְ אֶת־עֲפַר הָאָרֶץ וַתְּהִי הַכִּנָּם בָּאָדָם וּבַבְּהֵמָה
and in beast   in Adam   the lice   and it was   the earth   dust – that   and he smote

כָּל־עֲפַר הָאָרֶץ הָיָה כִנִּים בְּכָל־אֶרֶץ מִצְרָיִם:
Egypt   land – in all   lice   it was   the earth   dust – all

17 And they did so; for Aaron stretched out his hand with his rod, and smote the dust of the earth, and it became lice in man, and in beast; all the dust of the land became lice throughout all the land of Egypt.

וַיַּעֲשׂוּ־כֵן הַחַרְטֻמִּים בְּלָטֵיהֶם לְהוֹצִיא אֶת־הַכִּנִּים
the lice – that   to bring out   in their enchantments   the magicians   thus – and they did it

וְלֹא יָכֹלוּ וַתְּהִי הַכִּנָּם בָּאָדָם וּבַבְּהֵמָה:
and in beast   in Adam   the lice   and it was   they able   and not

18 And the magicians did so with their enchantments to bring forth lice, but they could not: so there were lice upon man, and upon beast.

וַיֹּאמְרוּ הַחַרְטֻמִּם אֶל־פַּרְעֹה אֶצְבַּע אֱלֹהִים הִוא
it   Elohim   finger   Pharaoh – unto   the magicians   and they said

וַיֶּחֱזַק לֵב־פַּרְעֹה
Pharaoh – heart   and he hardened

וְלֹא־שָׁמַע אֲלֵהֶם כַּאֲשֶׁר דִּבֶּר יְהוָה:
ihvh   spoke   when   unto them   heard – and not

19 Then the magicians said unto Pharaoh, This is the finger of God: and Pharaoh's heart was hardened, and he hearkened not unto them; as the LORD

had said.

ס

וַיֹּאמֶר יְהוָה אֶל־מֹשֶׁה הַשְׁכֵּם בַּבֹּקֶר
and he said   ihvh   Moses – unto   rise early you   in morning

וְהִתְיַצֵּב לִפְנֵי פַרְעֹה הִנֵּה יוֹצֵא הַמָּיְמָה
and cause to stand   before   Pharaoh   here   he comes out   the towards water

וְאָמַרְתָּ אֵלָיו כֹּה אָמַר יְהוָה שַׁלַּח עַמִּי וְיַעַבְדֻנִי:
and you say   unto him   thus   says   ihvh   send   my people   and they serve me

20 And the LORD said unto Moses, Rise up early in the morning, and stand before Pharaoh; lo, he cometh forth to the water; and say unto him, Thus saith the LORD, Let my people go, that they may serve me.

כִּי אִם־אֵינְךָ מְשַׁלֵּחַ אֶת־עַמִּי
like   if – isn't you   sender   that – my people

הִנְנִי מַשְׁלִיחַ בְּךָ וּבַעֲבָדֶיךָ וּבְעַמְּךָ וּבְבָתֶּיךָ
here I   sender   in you   and in your servant   and in your people   and in your house

אֶת־הֶעָרֹב
that – the flies

וּמָלְאוּ בָּתֵּי מִצְרַיִם אֶת־הֶעָרֹב
and they will fill   houses   Egyptians   that – the flies

וְגַם הָאֲדָמָה אֲשֶׁר־הֵם עָלֶיהָ:
and also   the ground   which – them   it ascends

21 Else, if thou wilt not let my people go, behold, I will send swarms of flies upon thee, and upon thy servants, and upon thy people, and into thy houses: and the houses of the Egyptians shall be full of swarms of flies, and also the ground whereon they are.

וְהִפְלֵיתִי בַיּוֹם הַהוּא אֶת־אֶרֶץ גֹּשֶׁן
and I will sever   in day   the it   that – land   Goshen

אֲשֶׁר עַמִּי עֹמֵד עָלֶיהָ לְבִלְתִּי הֱיוֹת־שָׁם עָרֹב לְמַעַן תֵּדַע
you know   to end   fly   there – to be   to be without   upon it   stand   my people   which

כִּי אֲנִי יְהוָה בְּקֶרֶב הָאָרֶץ:
like   I   ihvh   in midst   the earth

22 And I will sever in that day the land of Goshen, in which my people dwell, that no swarms of flies shall be there; to the end thou mayest know that I am the LORD in the midst of the earth.

[ששי]

וְשַׂמְתִּ֣י פְדֻ֔ת בֵּ֥ין עַמִּ֖י וּבֵ֣ין עַמֶּ֑ךָ
and I will put   division   between   my people   and between   your people

לְמָחָ֥ר יִהְיֶ֖ה הָאֹ֥ת הַזֶּֽה׃
to tomorrow   it will be   the sign   the this

23 And I will put a division between my people and thy people: tomorrow shall this sign be.

וַיַּ֤עַשׂ יְהֹוָה֙ כֵּ֔ן
and he did   ihvh   thus

וַיָּבֹא֙ עָרֹ֣ב כָּבֵ֔ד בֵּ֥יתָה פַרְעֹ֖ה וּבֵ֣ית עֲבָדָ֑יו
and it came   fly   heavy   house   Pharaoh   and house   his servants

וּבְכָל־אֶ֥רֶץ מִצְרַ֖יִם תִּשָּׁחֵ֥ת הָאָ֖רֶץ מִפְּנֵ֥י הֶעָרֹֽב׃
land – and in all   Egypt   it ruined   the land   from face   the fly

24 And the LORD did so; and there came a grievous swarm of flies into the house of Pharaoh, and into his servants' houses, and into all the land of Egypt: the land was corrupted by reason of the swarm of flies.

וַיִּקְרָ֣א פַרְעֹ֔ה אֶל־מֹשֶׁ֖ה וּֽלְאַהֲרֹ֑ן
and he called   Pharaoh   Moses – unto   and to Aaron

וַיֹּ֗אמֶר לְכ֛וּ זִבְח֥וּ לֵאלֹֽהֵיכֶ֖ם בָּאָֽרֶץ׃
in land   to your Elohim   you sacrifice   you go   and he said

25 And Pharaoh called for Moses and for Aaron, and said, Go ye, sacrifice to your God in the land.

וַיֹּ֣אמֶר מֹשֶׁ֗ה לֹ֤א נָכוֹן֙ לַעֲשׂ֣וֹת כֵּ֔ן
thus   to do   right   not   Moses   and he said

כִּ֚י תּוֹעֲבַ֣ת מִצְרַ֔יִם נִזְבַּ֖ח לַיהֹוָ֣ה אֱלֹהֵ֑ינוּ
our Elohim   to ihvh   we sacrifice   Egyptian   abomination   like

הֵ֣ן נִזְבַּ֞ח אֶת־תּוֹעֲבַ֥ת מִצְרַ֛יִם לְעֵינֵיהֶ֖ם וְלֹ֥א יִסְקְלֻֽנוּ׃
they stone us   and not   to their eyes   Egyptian   abomination – that   we will sacrifice   thus

26 And Moses said, It is not meet so to do; for we shall sacrifice the abomination of the Egyptians to the LORD our God: Lo, shall we sacrifice the abomination of the Egyptians before their eyes, and will they not stone us?

דֶּ֚רֶךְ שְׁלֹ֣שֶׁת יָמִ֔ים נֵלֵ֖ךְ בַּמִּדְבָּ֑ר
in wilderness   we go   days   three   way

וְזָבַ֖חְנוּ לַיהֹוָ֣ה אֱלֹהֵ֔ינוּ כַּאֲשֶׁ֖ר יֹאמַ֥ר אֵלֵֽינוּ׃
unto us   he says   when   our Elohim   to ihvh   and we sacrifice

27 We will go three days' journey into the wilderness, and sacrifice to the LORD our God, as he shall command us.

וַיֹּאמֶר פַּרְעֹה אָנֹכִי אֲשַׁלַּח אֶתְכֶם
that you   I will send   I am   Pharaoh   and he said

וּזְבַחְתֶּם לַיהוָה אֱלֹהֵיכֶם בַּמִּדְבָּר
in wilderness   your Elohim   to ihvh   and you sacrifice

רַק הַרְחֵק לֹא־תַרְחִיקוּ לָלֶכֶת הַעְתִּירוּ בַּעֲדִי׃
in myself   the entreat you   to go   you far it – not   the far   only

28 And Pharaoh said, I will let you go, that ye may sacrifice to the LORD your God in the wilderness; only ye shall not go very far away: entreat for me.

וַיֹּאמֶר מֹשֶׁה הִנֵּה אָנֹכִי יוֹצֵא מֵעִמָּךְ
from with you   come out   I am   here   Moses   and he said

וְהַעְתַּרְתִּי אֶל־יְהוָה
ihvh – unto   and the I entreat

וְסָר הֶעָרֹב מִפַּרְעֹה מֵעֲבָדָיו וּמֵעַמּוֹ מָחָר
tomorrow   and from his people   from his servants   from Pharaoh   the flies   and depart

רַק אַל־יֹסֵף פַּרְעֹה הָתֵל לְבִלְתִּי
to without   tifleing   Pharaoh   he add – don't   only

שַׁלַּח אֶת־הָעָם לִזְבֹּחַ לַיהוָה׃
to ihvh   to sacrifice   the people – that   send

29 And Moses said, Behold, I go out from thee, and I will entreat the LORD that the swarms of flies may depart from Pharaoh, from his servants, and from his people, tomorrow: but let not Pharaoh deal deceitfully any more in not letting the people go to sacrifice to the LORD.

וַיֵּצֵא מֹשֶׁה מֵעִם פַּרְעֹה וַיֶּעְתַּר אֶל־יְהוָה׃
ihvh – unto   and he entreated   Pharaoh   from with   Moses   and he went out

30 And Moses went out from Pharaoh, and entreated the LORD.

וַיַּעַשׂ יְהוָה כִּדְבַר מֹשֶׁה
Moses   like spoke   ihvh   and he did

וַיָּסַר הֶעָרֹב מִפַּרְעֹה מֵעֲבָדָיו וּמֵעַמּוֹ
and from his people   from his servants   from Pharaoh   the flies   and he removed

לֹא נִשְׁאַר אֶחָד׃
one   remained   not

31 And the LORD did according to the word of Moses; and he removed the swarms of flies from Pharaoh, from his servants, and from his people; there remained not one.

וַיַּכְבֵּד פַּרְעֹה אֶת־לִבּוֹ גַּם בַּפַּעַם הַזֹּאת
the this   in time   also   his heart – that   Pharaoh   and he heavy

וְלֹא שִׁלַּח אֶת־הָעָם:
the people – that   send   and not

32 And Pharaoh hardened his heart at this time also, neither would he let the people go.

CHAPTER 9

ספר שמות פרק ט

וַיֹּאמֶר יְהֹוָה אֶל־מֹשֶׁה בֹּא אֶל־פַּרְעֹה
Pharaoh – unto   come   Moses – unto   ihvh   and he said

וְדִבַּרְתָּ אֵלָיו כֹּה־אָמַר יְהֹוָה אֱלֹהֵי הָעִבְרִים
the Hebrews   Elohim   ihvh   says – thus   unto him   and you speak

שַׁלַּח אֶת־עַמִּי וְיַעַבְדֻנִי:
and they serve me   my people – that   send

1 Then the LORD said unto Moses, Go in unto Pharaoh, and tell him, Thus saith the LORD God of the Hebrews, Let my people go, that they may serve me.

כִּי אִם־מָאֵן אַתָּה לְשַׁלֵּחַ וְעוֹדְךָ מַחֲזִיק בָּם:
in them   hold   and you still   to send   you   refuse – with   like

2 For if thou refuse to let them go, and wilt hold them still,

הִנֵּה יַד־יְהֹוָה הוֹיָה בְּמִקְנְךָ אֲשֶׁר בַּשָּׂדֶה
in field   which   in your cattle   doer   ihvh – hand   here

בַּסּוּסִים בַּחֲמֹרִים בַּגְּמַלִּים בַּבָּקָר וּבַצֹּאן
and in sheep   in oxen   in camels   in asses   in horses

דֶּבֶר כָּבֵד מְאֹד:
very   heavy   will be pestilence

3 Behold, the hand of the LORD is upon thy cattle which is in the field, upon the horses, upon the asses, upon the camels, upon the oxen, and upon the sheep: there shall be a very grievous murrain.

וְהִפְלָה יְהֹוָה בֵּין מִקְנֵה יִשְׂרָאֵל
Israel   cattle   between   ihvh   and will sever

וּבֵין מִקְנֵה מִצְרָיִם
Egyptians   cattle   and between

וְלֹא יָמוּת מִכָּל־לִבְנֵי יִשְׂרָאֵל דָּבָר:
matter   Israel   to sons – from all   they will die   and not

4 And the LORD shall sever between the cattle of Israel and the cattle of Egypt: and there shall nothing die of all that is the children's of Israel.

וַיָּשֶׂם יְהֹוָה מוֹעֵד לֵאמֹר
to say   appointed time   ihvh   and he set

מָחָר יַעֲשֶׂה יְהוָה הַדָּבָר הַזֶּה בָּאָרֶץ:
in land   the this   the matter   ihvh   he will do   tomorrow

5 And the LORD appointed a set time, saying, Tomorrow the LORD shall do this thing in the land.

וַיַּעַשׂ יְהוָה אֶת־הַדָּבָר הַזֶּה מִמָּחֳרָת
from next day   the this   the matter – that   ihvh   and he did

וַיָּמָת כֹּל מִקְנֵה מִצְרָיִם
Egyptians   cattle   all   and it died

וּמִמִּקְנֵה בְנֵי־יִשְׂרָאֵל לֹא־מֵת אֶחָד:
one   died – not   Israel – sons   and from cattle

6 And the LORD did that thing on the morrow, and all the cattle of Egypt died: but of the cattle of the children of Israel died not one.

וַיִּשְׁלַח פַּרְעֹה וְהִנֵּה לֹא־מֵת מִמִּקְנֵה יִשְׂרָאֵל עַד־אֶחָד
one – till   Israel   from cattle   died – not   and here   Pharaoh   and he sent

וַיִּכְבַּד לֵב פַּרְעֹה וְלֹא שִׁלַּח אֶת־הָעָם:
the people – that   send   and not   Pharaoh   heart   and he heavy

7 And Pharaoh sent, and, behold, there was not one of the cattle of the Israelites dead. And the heart of Pharaoh was hardened, and he did not let the people go.

פ

וַיֹּאמֶר יְהוָה אֶל־מֹשֶׁה וְאֶל־אַהֲרֹן
Aaron – and unto   Moses – unto   ihvh   and he said

קְחוּ לָכֶם מְלֹא חָפְנֵיכֶם פִּיחַ כִּבְשָׁן
lime kiln   ash   your both hands   full   to you   you take

וּזְרָקוֹ מֹשֶׁה הַשָּׁמַיְמָה לְעֵינֵי פַרְעֹה:
Pharaoh   to eyes   the towards heaven   Moses   and his sprinkle

8 And the LORD said unto Moses and unto Aaron, Take to you handfuls of ashes of the furnace, and let Moses sprinkle it toward the heaven in the sight of Pharaoh.

וְהָיָה לְאָבָק עַל כָּל־אֶרֶץ מִצְרָיִם
Egypt   land – all   upon   to fine dust   and it was

וְהָיָה עַל־הָאָדָם וְעַל־הַבְּהֵמָה לִשְׁחִין
to boils   the beast - and upon   the Adam – upon   and it was

פֹּרֵחַ אֲבַעְבֻּעֹת בְּכָל־אֶרֶץ מִצְרָיִם:
Egypt   land – in all   pustules   breaking forth

9 And it shall become small dust in all the land of Egypt, and shall be a boil breaking forth with blains upon man, and upon beast, throughout all the land

of Egypt.

וַיִּקְחוּ אֶת־פִּיחַ הַכִּבְשָׁן וַיַּעַמְדוּ לִפְנֵי פַרְעֹה
and he took it   that – ash   the lime kiln   and they stood   before   Pharaoh

וַיִּזְרֹק אֹתוֹ מֹשֶׁה הַשָּׁמָיְמָה
and he sprinkled   to it   Moses   the towards heaven

וַיְהִי שְׁחִין אֲבַעְבֻּעֹת פֹּרֵחַ בָּאָדָם וּבַבְּהֵמָה׃
and it was   boils   blains   broke out   in Adam   and in beast

10 And they took ashes of the furnace, and stood before Pharaoh; and Moses sprinkled it up toward heaven; and it became a boil breaking forth with blains upon man, and upon beast.

וְלֹא־יָכְלוּ הַחַרְטֻמִּים לַעֲמֹד לִפְנֵי מֹשֶׁה מִפְּנֵי הַשְּׁחִין
and not – they able   the magicians   to stand   before   Moses   from before   the boils

כִּי־הָיָה הַשְּׁחִין בַּחַרְטֻמִּם וּבְכָל־מִצְרָיִם׃
like – it was   the boils   in magicians   and in all – Egyptians

11 And the magicians could not stand before Moses because of the boils; for the boil was upon the magicians, and upon all the Egyptians.

וַיְחַזֵּק יְהֹוָה אֶת־לֵב פַּרְעֹה
and strengthened   ihvh   that – heart   Pharaoh

וְלֹא שָׁמַע אֲלֵהֶם כַּאֲשֶׁר דִּבֶּר יְהֹוָה אֶל־מֹשֶׁה׃
and not   heard   unto them   when   spoke   ihvh   unto - Moses

12 And the LORD hardened the heart of Pharaoh, and he hearkened not unto them; as the LORD had spoken unto Moses.

ס

וַיֹּאמֶר יְהֹוָה אֶל־מֹשֶׁה הַשְׁכֵּם בַּבֹּקֶר
and he said   ihvh   unto – Moses   you rise early   in morning

וְהִתְיַצֵּב לִפְנֵי פַרְעֹה וְאָמַרְתָּ אֵלָיו
and cause to stand   before   Pharaoh   and you say   unto him

כֹּה־אָמַר יְהֹוָה אֱלֹהֵי הָעִבְרִים שַׁלַּח אֶת־עַמִּי וְיַעַבְדֻנִי׃
thus – says   ihvh   Elohim   the Hebrews   send   that – my people   and they serve me

13 And the LORD said unto Moses, Rise up early in the morning, and stand before Pharaoh, and say unto him, Thus saith the LORD God of the Hebrews, Let my people go, that they may serve me.

כִּי בַּפַּעַם הַזֹּאת אֲנִי שֹׁלֵחַ אֶת־כָּל־מַגֵּפֹתַי
like   in times   the this   I   will send   that – all – my plagues

אֶל־לִבְּךָ וּבַעֲבָדֶיךָ וּבְעַמֶּךָ
unto – your heart   and in your servants   and in your people

PARASHAT 2   CHAPTER 9   69

בַּעֲב֣וּר תֵּדַ֔ע כִּ֛י אֵ֥ין כָּמֹ֖נִי בְּכָל־הָאָֽרֶץ׃
     the earth – in all like me isn't like you know in sake

14 For I will at this time send all my plagues upon thine heart, and upon thy servants, and upon thy people; that thou mayest know that there is none like me in all the earth.

כִּ֤י עַתָּה֙ שָׁלַ֣חְתִּי אֶת־יָדִ֔י וָאַ֥ךְ אוֹתְךָ֖
to you and smite my hand – that I will send now like

וְאֶֽת־עַמְּךָ֖ בַּדָּ֑בֶר וַתִּכָּחֵ֖ד מִן־הָאָֽרֶץ׃
the earth – from and you will be cut off in pestilence your people – and that

15 For now I will stretch out my hand, that I may smite thee and thy people with pestilence; and thou shalt be cut off from the earth.

וְאוּלָ֗ם בַּעֲב֥וּר זֹאת֙ הֶעֱמַדְתִּ֔יךָ בַּעֲב֖וּר הַרְאֹתְךָ֣ אֶת־כֹּחִ֑י
my power-that the your badness in sake the I stood you this in sake and perhaps

וּלְמַ֛עַן סַפֵּ֥ר שְׁמִ֖י בְּכָל־הָאָֽרֶץ׃
the earth - in all my name story and to end

16 And in very deed for this cause have I raised thee up, for to shew in thee my power; and that my name may be declared throughout all the earth.

[שביעי]

עוֹדְךָ֖ מִסְתּוֹלֵ֣ל בְּעַמִּ֑י לְבִלְתִּ֖י שַׁלְּחָֽם׃
send them to without in my people heap up still you

17 As yet exaltest thou thyself against my people, that thou wilt not let them go?

הִנְנִ֤י מַמְטִיר֙ כָּעֵ֣ת מָחָ֔ר בָּרָ֖ד כָּבֵ֣ד מְאֹ֑ד
great heavy hail tomorrow like time from rain here

אֲשֶׁ֨ר לֹֽא־הָיָ֤ה כָמֹ֙הוּ֙ בְּמִצְרַ֔יִם
in Egypt like it it was – not which

לְמִן־הַיּ֥וֹם הִוָּסְדָ֖ה וְעַד־עָֽתָּה׃
now – and till set foundation the day – to from

18 Behold, tomorrow about this time I will cause it to rain a very grievous hail, such as hath not been in Egypt since the foundation thereof even until now.

וְעַתָּ֗ה שְׁלַ֤ח הָעֵז֙ אֶֽת־מִקְנְךָ֔
your cattle – that the barn send and now

וְאֵ֛ת כָּל־אֲשֶׁ֥ר לְךָ֖ בַּשָּׂדֶ֑ה
in field to you which – all and that

כָּל־הָאָדָ֨ם וְהַבְּהֵמָ֜ה אֲשֶֽׁר־יִמָּצֵ֣א בַשָּׂדֶ֗ה
in field he will find – which and the beast the Adam – all

וְלֹא יֵאָסֵף הַבַּיְתָה
and not   he will gather   the house ward

וְיָרַד עֲלֵהֶם הַבָּרָד וָמֵתוּ׃
and it will come down   upon them   the hail   and it will die

19 Send therefore now, and gather thy cattle, and all that thou hast in the field; for upon every man and beast which shall be found in the field, and shall not be brought home, the hail shall come down upon them, and they shall die.

הַיָּרֵא אֶת־דְּבַר יְהוָה מֵעַבְדֵי פַּרְעֹה הֵנִיס אֶת־עֲבָדָיו
the he feared   speech – that   ihvh   from servants   Pharaoh   caused flee   his servants – that

וְאֶת־מִקְנֵהוּ אֶל־הַבָּתִּים׃
his cattle – and that   the houses – unto

20 He that feared the word of the LORD among the servants of Pharaoh made his servants and his cattle flee into the houses:

וַאֲשֶׁר לֹא־שָׂם לִבּוֹ אֶל־דְּבַר יְהוָה
and which   not – put   his heart   unto – speak   ihvh

וַיַּעֲזֹב אֶת־עֲבָדָיו וְאֶת־מִקְנֵהוּ בַּשָּׂדֶה׃
and he left   his servants – that   his cattle – and that   in field

21 And he that regarded not the word of the LORD left his servants and his cattle in the field.

פ

וַיֹּאמֶר יְהוָה אֶל־מֹשֶׁה נְטֵה אֶת־יָדְךָ עַל־הַשָּׁמַיִם
and he said   ihvh   Moses – unto   stretch out   your hand – that   the heavens – upon

וִיהִי בָרָד בְּכָל־אֶרֶץ מִצְרַיִם עַל־הָאָדָם
and it will be   hail   land – in all   Egypt   the Adam – upon

וְעַל־הַבְּהֵמָה וְעַל כָּל־עֵשֶׂב הַשָּׂדֶה בְּאֶרֶץ מִצְרָיִם׃
the beast – and upon   and upon   grass – all   the field   in land   Egypt

22 And the LORD said unto Moses, Stretch forth thine hand toward heaven, that there may be hail in all the land of Egypt, upon man, and upon beast, and upon every herb of the field, throughout the land of Egypt.

וַיֵּט מֹשֶׁה אֶת־מַטֵּהוּ עַל־הַשָּׁמַיִם
and he stretched out   Moses   his rod – that   the heavens – upon

וַיהוָה נָתַן קֹלֹת וּבָרָד וַתִּהֲלַךְ־אֵשׁ אָרְצָה
and ihvh   gave   thunders   and hail   fire – and it went   towards ground

וַיַּמְטֵר יְהוָה בָּרָד עַל־אֶרֶץ מִצְרָיִם׃
and he rained   ihvh   hail   land – upon   Egypt

23 And Moses stretched forth his rod toward heaven: and the LORD sent thunder and hail, and the fire ran along upon the ground; and the LORD rained hail upon the land of Egypt.

וַיְהִ֣י בָרָ֔ד וְאֵ֕שׁ מִתְלַקַּ֖חַת בְּת֣וֹךְ הַבָּרָ֑ד כָּבֵ֥ד מְאֹ֖ד
very　heavy　the hail　in midst　from taking itself　and fire　hail　and there was

אֲשֶׁ֨ר לֹֽא־הָיָ֤ה כָמֹ֙הוּ֙ בְּכָל־אֶ֣רֶץ מִצְרַ֔יִם מֵאָ֖ז הָיְתָ֥ה לְגֽוֹי׃
to nation　it was　from then　Egypt　land – in all　like it　was - not　which

24 So there was hail, and fire mingled with the hail, very grievous, such as there was none like it in all the land of Egypt since it became a nation.

וַיַּ֤ךְ הַבָּרָד֙ בְּכָל־אֶ֣רֶץ מִצְרַ֔יִם
Egypt　land – in all　the hail　and it smote

אֵ֛ת כָּל־אֲשֶׁ֥ר בַּשָּׂדֶ֖ה מֵאָדָ֣ם וְעַד־בְּהֵמָ֑ה
beast – and till　from Adam　in field　which – all　that

וְאֵ֨ת כָּל־עֵ֤שֶׂב הַשָּׂדֶה֙ הִכָּ֣ה הַבָּרָ֔ד
the hail　smote　the field　grass – all　and that

וְאֶת־כָּל־עֵ֥ץ הַשָּׂדֶ֖ה שִׁבֵּֽר׃
broke　the field　tree - all - and that

25 And the hail smote throughout all the land of Egypt all that was in the field, both man and beast; and the hail smote every herb of the field, and brake every tree of the field.

רַ֚ק בְּאֶ֣רֶץ גֹּ֔שֶׁן אֲשֶׁר־שָׁ֖ם בְּנֵ֣י יִשְׂרָאֵ֑ל לֹ֥א הָיָ֖ה בָּרָֽד׃
hail　it was　not　Israel　sons　there – which　Goshen　in land　only

26 Only in the land of Goshen, where the children of Israel were, was there no hail.

וַיִּשְׁלַ֣ח פַּרְעֹ֗ה וַיִּקְרָא֙ לְמֹשֶׁ֣ה וּֽלְאַהֲרֹ֔ן
and to Aaron　to Moses　and he called　Pharaoh　and he sent

וַיֹּ֤אמֶר אֲלֵהֶם֙ חָטָ֣אתִי הַפָּ֑עַם יְהוָה֙ הַצַּדִּ֔יק
the righteous　ihvh　the again time　I sinned　unto them　and he said

וַאֲנִ֥י וְעַמִּ֖י הָרְשָׁעִֽים׃
the wicked ones　and my people　and I

27 And Pharaoh sent, and called for Moses and Aaron, and said unto them, I have sinned this time: the LORD is righteous, and I and my people are wicked.

הַעְתִּ֙ירוּ֙ אֶל־יְהוָ֔ה וְרַ֕ב מִֽהְיֹ֛ת קֹלֹ֥ת אֱלֹהִ֖ים וּבָרָ֑ד
and hail　Elohim　thundering　from being　and much　ihvh – unto　the you entreat

וַאֲשַׁלְּחָ֣ה אֶתְכֶ֔ם וְלֹ֥א תֹסִפ֖וּן לַעֲמֹֽד׃
to stand　you will remain　and not　that you　and I will send

PARASHAT 2　CHAPTER 9

28 Entreat the LORD (for it is enough) that there be no more mighty thunderings and hail; and I will let you go, and ye shall stay no longer.

וַיֹּאמֶר אֵלָיו מֹשֶׁה כְּצֵאתִי אֶת־הָעִיר
the city – that   like I go out   Moses   unto him   and he said

אֶפְרֹשׂ אֶת־כַּפַּי אֶל־יְהֹוָה
ihvh – unto   my palms – that   I spread

הַקֹּלוֹת יֶחְדָּלוּן וְהַבָּרָד לֹא יִהְיֶה־עוֹד
again – it will be   not   and the hail   it will cease   the thundering

לְמַעַן תֵּדַע כִּי לַיהֹוָה הָאָרֶץ׃
the earth   to ihvh   like   you know   to end

29 And Moses said unto him, As soon as I am gone out of the city, I will spread abroad my hands unto the LORD; and the thunder shall cease, neither shall there be any more hail; that thou mayest know how that the earth is the LORD'S.

וְאַתָּה וַעֲבָדֶיךָ יָדַעְתִּי
I know   and your servants   and you

כִּי טֶרֶם תִּירְאוּן מִפְּנֵי יְהֹוָה אֱלֹהִים׃
Elohim   ihvh   from face   you will fear   not yet   like

30 But as for thee and thy servants, I know that ye will not yet fear the LORD God.

וְהַפִּשְׁתָּה וְהַשְּׂעֹרָה נֻכָּתָה כִּי הַשְּׂעֹרָה אָבִיב
pollinated   the barley   like   smitten   and the barley   and the flax

וְהַפִּשְׁתָּה גִּבְעֹל׃
encased pod   and the flax

31 And the flax and the barley was smitten: for the barley was in the ear, and the flax was bolled.

וְהַחִטָּה וְהַכֻּסֶּמֶת לֹא נֻכּוּ כִּי אֲפִילֹת הֵנָּה׃
here   in blade   like   smitten   not   and the spelt   and the wheat

32 But the wheat and the rie were not smitten: for they were not grown up.

[מפטיר]

וַיֵּצֵא מֹשֶׁה מֵעִם פַּרְעֹה אֶת־הָעִיר
the city – that   Pharaoh   from with   Moses   and he went out

וַיִּפְרֹשׂ כַּפָּיו אֶל־יְהֹוָה
ihvh – unto   his palms   and he spread

וַיַּחְדְּלוּ הַקֹּלוֹת וְהַבָּרָד וּמָטָר לֹא־נִתַּךְ אָרְצָה׃
towards earth   poured – not   and rain   and the hail   the thundering   and they ceased

PARASHAT 2   CHAPTER 9

33 And Moses went out of the city from Pharaoh, and spread abroad his hands unto the LORD: and the thunders and hail ceased, and the rain was not poured upon the earth.

וַיֵּרָא פַרְעֹה כִּי־חָדַל הַמָּטָר וְהַבָּרָד וְהַקֹּלֹת
and he saw   Pharaoh   like - ceased   the rain   and the hail   and the thundering

וַיֹּסֶף לַחֲטֹא
and he added   to sin

וַיַּכְבֵּד לִבּוֹ הוּא וַעֲבָדָיו׃
and he heavy   his heart   he   and his servants

34 And when Pharaoh saw that the rain and the hail and the thunders were ceased, he sinned yet more, and hardened his heart, he and his servants.

וַיֶּחֱזַק לֵב פַּרְעֹה
and he hardened   heart   Pharaoh

וְלֹא שִׁלַּח אֶת־בְּנֵי יִשְׂרָאֵל כַּאֲשֶׁר דִּבֶּר יְהוָה בְּיַד־מֹשֶׁה׃
and not   sent   that - sons   Israel   when   spoke   ihvh   in hand - Moses

35 And the heart of Pharaoh was hardened, neither would he let the children of Israel go; as the LORD had spoken by Moses.

פ פ פ

PARASHAT 3 - BO

CHAPTER 10

[פרשת בא]

ספר שמות פרק י

וַיֹּאמֶר יְהוָה אֶל־מֹשֶׁה בֹּא אֶל־פַּרְעֹה
    Pharaoh – unto   come   Moses – unto   ihvh   and he said

כִּי־אֲנִי הִכְבַּדְתִּי אֶת־לִבּוֹ וְאֶת־לֵב עֲבָדָיו
his servants   heart – and that   his heart – that   caused to be heavy   I – like

לְמַעַן שִׁתִי אֹתֹתַי אֵלֶּה בְּקִרְבּוֹ׃
in his close   these   my signs   I set   to end

1 And the LORD said unto Moses, Go in unto Pharaoh: for I have hardened his heart, and the heart of his servants, that I might shew these my signs before him:

וּלְמַעַן תְּסַפֵּר בְּאָזְנֵי בִנְךָ
your son   in ears   you story   and to end

וּבֶן־בִּנְךָ אֵת אֲשֶׁר הִתְעַלַּלְתִּי בְּמִצְרַיִם
in Egypt   I caused to curse   which   that   your son – and son

וְאֶת־אֹתֹתַי אֲשֶׁר־שַׂמְתִּי בָם
in them   I put - which   my signs - and that

וִידַעְתֶּם כִּי־אֲנִי יְהוָה׃
ihvh   I – like   and you know

2 And that thou mayest tell in the ears of thy son, and of thy son's son, what things I have wrought in Egypt, and my signs which I have done among them; that ye may know how that I am the LORD.

וַיָּבֹא מֹשֶׁה וְאַהֲרֹן אֶל־פַּרְעֹה
Pharaoh – unto   and Aaron   Moses   and he came

וַיֹּאמְרוּ אֵלָיו כֹּה־אָמַר יְהוָה אֱלֹהֵי הָעִבְרִים
the Hebrews   Elohim   ihvh   says – thus   unto him   and they said

עַד־מָתַי מֵאַנְתָּ לֵעָנֹת מִפָּנָי
from my face   to humble   you refuse   when – till

שַׁלַּח עַמִּי וְיַעַבְדֻנִי׃
and they serve me   my people   send

3 And Moses and Aaron came in unto Pharaoh, and said unto him, Thus saith the LORD God of the Hebrews, How long wilt thou refuse to humble thyself

before me? let my people go, that they may serve me.

כִּי אִם־מָאֵן אַתָּה לְשַׁלֵּחַ אֶת־עַמִּי

like   refuse – with   you   to send   my people – that

הִנְנִי מֵבִיא מָחָר אַרְבֶּה בִּגְבֻלֶךָ:

here I   will bring   tomorrow   locusts   in your borders

4 Else, if thou refuse to let my people go, behold, tomorrow will I bring the locusts into thy coast:

וְכִסָּה אֶת־עֵין הָאָרֶץ

and will cover   eye – that   the earth

וְלֹא יוּכַל לִרְאֹת אֶת־הָאָרֶץ

and not   he able   to see   the earth – that

וְאָכַל אֶת־יֶתֶר הַפְּלֵטָה הַנִּשְׁאֶרֶת לָכֶם מִן־הַבָּרָד

and will eat   remnant – that   to you   the remainder   the escaped   the hail – from

וְאָכַל אֶת־כָּל־הָעֵץ הַצֹּמֵחַ לָכֶם מִן־הַשָּׂדֶה:

and will eat   the tree – all – that   the growth   to you   the field – from

5 And they shall cover the face of the earth, that one cannot be able to see the earth: and they shall eat the residue of that which is escaped, which remaineth unto you from the hail, and shall eat every tree which groweth for you out of the field:

וּמָלְאוּ בָתֶּיךָ וּבָתֵּי כָל־עֲבָדֶיךָ וּבָתֵּי כָל־מִצְרַיִם

Egyptians – all   and houses   your servant – all   and house   your house   and they will fill

אֲשֶׁר לֹא־רָאוּ אֲבֹתֶיךָ וַאֲבוֹת אֲבֹתֶיךָ

which   they saw – not   your fathers   and fathers   your fathers

מִיּוֹם הֱיוֹתָם עַל־הָאֲדָמָה עַד הַיּוֹם הַזֶּה

from day   they were   the ground – upon   till   the day   the this

וַיִּפֶן וַיֵּצֵא מֵעִם פַּרְעֹה:

and he turned   and he went out   from with   Pharaoh

6 And they shall fill thy houses, and the houses of all thy servants, and the houses of all the Egyptians; which neither thy fathers, nor thy fathers' fathers have seen, since the day that they were upon the earth unto this day. And he turned himself, and went out from Pharaoh.

וַיֹּאמְרוּ עַבְדֵי פַרְעֹה אֵלָיו

and they said   servants   Pharaoh   unto him

עַד־מָתַי יִהְיֶה זֶה לָנוּ לְמוֹקֵשׁ

when – till   it was   this   to us   to trap

שְׁלַח	אֶת־הָאֲנָשִׁים	וְיַעַבְדוּ	אֶת־יְהוָֹה	אֱלֹהֵיהֶם
send	the men – that	and they serve	ihvh – that	their Elohim

הֲטֶרֶם	תֵּדַע	כִּי	אָבְדָה	מִצְרָיִם:
the yet	you know	like	destroyed	Egypt

7 And Pharaoh's servants said unto him, How long shall this man be a snare unto us? let the men go, that they may serve the LORD their God: knowest thou not yet that Egypt is destroyed?

וַיּוּשַׁב	אֶת־מֹשֶׁה	וְאֶת־אַהֲרֹן	אֶל־פַּרְעֹה
and he returned	Moses – that	Aaron - and that	Pharaoh – unto

וַיֹּאמֶר	אֲלֵהֶם	לְכוּ	עִבְדוּ	אֶת־יְהוָֹה	אֱלֹהֵיכֶם
and he said	unto them	you go	you serve	ihvh – that	your Elohim

מִי	וָמִי	הַהֹלְכִים:
who	and who	the going ones

8 And Moses and Aaron were brought again unto Pharaoh: and he said unto them, Go, serve the LORD your God: but who are they that shall go?

וַיֹּאמֶר	מֹשֶׁה	בִּנְעָרֵינוּ	וּבִזְקֵנֵינוּ
and he said	Moses	in our young ones	and in our old ones

נֵלֵךְ	בְּבָנֵינוּ	וּבִבְנוֹתֵנוּ
we go	in our sons	and in our daughters

בְּצֹאנֵנוּ	וּבִבְקָרֵנוּ	נֵלֵךְ	כִּי	חַג־יְהוָֹה	לָנוּ:
in our sheep	and in our cattle	we go	like	ihvh – feast	to us

9 And Moses said, We will go with our young and with our old, with our sons and with our daughters, with our flocks and with our herds will we go; for we must hold a feast unto the LORD.

וַיֹּאמֶר	אֲלֵהֶם	יְהִי	כֵן	יְהוָֹה	עִמָּכֶם	כַּאֲשֶׁר	אֲשַׁלַּח	אֶתְכֶם
and he said	unto them	it be	thus	ihvh	with you	when	I will send	that you

וְאֶת־טַפְּכֶם
your little ones - and that

רְאוּ	כִּי	רָעָה	נֶגֶד	פְּנֵיכֶם:
you see	like	bad	before	your faces

10 And he said unto them, Let the LORD be so with you, as I will let you go, and your little ones: look to it; for evil is before you.

לֹא	כֵן	לְכוּ־נָא	הַגְּבָרִים	וְעִבְדוּ	אֶת־יְהוָֹה
not	thus	now – you go	the men	and you serve	ihvh – that

כִּי	אֹתָהּ	אַתֶּם	מְבַקְשִׁים
like	to that	you	requesting ones

וַיְגָ֧רֶשׁ   אֹתָ֖ם   מֵאֵ֥ת פְּנֵ֥י פַרְעֹֽה׃
and he drove out   to them   from that   face   Pharaoh

11 Not so: go now ye that are men, and serve the LORD; for that ye did desire. And they were driven out from Pharaoh's presence.

ס
[שני]

וַיֹּ֨אמֶר יְהֹוָ֜ה אֶל־מֹשֶׁ֗ה נְטֵ֤ה יָֽדְךָ֙ עַל־אֶ֣רֶץ מִצְרַ֔יִם בָּאַרְבֶּ֔ה
in locusts   Egypt   land - upon   your hand   stretch out   Moses – unto   ihvh   and he said

וְיַ֖עַל עַל־אֶ֣רֶץ מִצְרָ֑יִם
Egypt   land – upon   and it ascend

וְיֹאכַל֙ אֶת־כָּל־עֵ֣שֶׂב הָאָ֔רֶץ אֵ֛ת כָּל־אֲשֶׁ֥ר הִשְׁאִ֖יר הַבָּרָֽד׃
the hail   remained   which – all   that   the land   grass – all – that   and it eat

12 And the LORD said unto Moses, Stretch out thine hand over the land of Egypt for the locusts, that they may come up upon the land of Egypt, and eat every herb of the land, even all that the hail hath left.

וַיֵּ֨ט מֹשֶׁ֣ה אֶת־מַטֵּ֘הוּ֮ עַל־אֶ֣רֶץ מִצְרַ֗יִם
Egypt   land – upon   his rod – that   Moses   and he stretched out

וַֽיהֹוָ֗ה נִהַ֤ג רֽוּחַ־קָדִים֙ בָּאָ֔רֶץ כָּל־הַיּ֥וֹם הַה֖וּא
the it   the day – all   in land   east – wind   drove   and ihvh

וְכָל־הַלָּ֑יְלָה הַבֹּ֣קֶר הָיָ֔ה
it was   the morning   the night – and all

וְר֙וּחַ֙ הַקָּדִ֔ים נָשָׂ֖א אֶת־הָאַרְבֶּֽה׃
the locust – that   lifted   the east   and wind

13 And Moses stretched forth his rod over the land of Egypt, and the LORD brought an east wind upon the land all that day, and all that night; and when it was morning, the east wind brought the locusts.

וַיַּ֣עַל הָֽאַרְבֶּ֗ה עַ֚ל כָּל־אֶ֣רֶץ מִצְרַ֔יִם
Egypt   land – all   upon   the locust   and it ascended

וַיָּ֕נַח בְּכֹ֖ל גְּב֣וּל מִצְרָ֑יִם כָּבֵ֣ד מְאֹ֔ד
very   heavy   Egypt   borders   in all   and it rested

לְפָנָ֗יו לֹא־הָ֤יָה כֵן֙ אַרְבֶּ֣ה כָּמֹ֔הוּ
like it   locust   thus   it was – not   before him

וְאַחֲרָ֖יו לֹ֥א יִֽהְיֶה־כֵּֽן׃
thus – it was   not   and after it

14 And the locusts went up over all the land of Egypt, and rested in all the coasts of Egypt: very grievous were they; before them there were no such locusts as they, neither after them shall be such.

וַיְכַס אֶת־עֵין כָּל־הָאָרֶץ וַתֶּחְשַׁךְ הָאָרֶץ
the land   and it darkened   the earth – all   eye – that   and it covered

וַיֹּאכַל אֶת־כָּל־עֵשֶׂב הָאָרֶץ
the land   grass – all – that   and it ate

וְאֵת כָּל־פְּרִי הָעֵץ אֲשֶׁר הוֹתִיר הַבָּרָד
the hail   remained   which   the tree   fruit – all   and that

וְלֹא־נוֹתַר כָּל־יֶרֶק בָּעֵץ
in tree   green – all   remained – and not

וּבְעֵשֶׂב הַשָּׂדֶה בְּכָל־אֶרֶץ מִצְרָיִם:
Egypt   land – in all   the field   and in grass

15 For they covered the face of the whole earth, so that the land was darkened; and they did eat every herb of the land, and all the fruit of the trees which the hail had left: and there remained not any green thing in the trees, or in the herbs of the field, through all the land of Egypt.

וַיְמַהֵר פַּרְעֹה לִקְרֹא לְמֹשֶׁה וּלְאַהֲרֹן
and to Aaron   to Moses   to call   Pharaoh   and he hurried

וַיֹּאמֶר חָטָאתִי לַיהוָה אֱלֹהֵיכֶם וְלָכֶם:
and to you   your Elohim   to ihvh   I sinned   and he said

16 Then Pharaoh called for Moses and Aaron in haste; and he said, I have sinned against the LORD your God, and against you.

וְעַתָּה שָׂא נָא חַטָּאתִי אַךְ הַפַּעַם
the once   only   my sin   now   lift   and now

וְהַעְתִּירוּ לַיהוָה אֱלֹהֵיכֶם
your Elohim   to ihvh   and the you entreat

וְיָסֵר מֵעָלַי רַק אֶת־הַמָּוֶת הַזֶּה:
the thus   the death – that   only   from upon me   and he remove

17 Now therefore forgive, I pray thee, my sin only this once, and entreat the LORD your God, that he may take away from me this death only.

וַיֵּצֵא מֵעִם פַּרְעֹה וַיֶּעְתַּר אֶל־יְהוָה:
ihvh – unto   and he entreated   Pharaoh   from with   and he went out

18 And he went out from Pharaoh, and entreated the LORD.

וַיַּהֲפֹךְ יְהוָה רוּחַ־יָם חָזָק מְאֹד
great   mighty   sea – wind   ihvh   and he turned

וַיִּשָּׂא אֶת־הָאַרְבֶּה וַיִּתְקָעֵהוּ יָמָּה סּוּף
end   towards sea   and he blew it   the locust – that   and he lifted

לֹא נִשְׁאַר אַרְבֶּה אֶחָד בְּכֹל גְּבוּל מִצְרָיִם:
    Egypt   borders   in all   one   locust   remained   not

19 And the LORD turned a mighty strong west wind, which took away the locusts, and cast them into the Red sea; there remained not one locust in all the coasts of Egypt.

וַיְחַזֵּק יְהוָה אֶת־לֵב פַּרְעֹה
    Pharaoh   heart – that   ihvh   and he hardened

וְלֹא שִׁלַּח אֶת־בְּנֵי יִשְׂרָאֵל:
    Israel   sons – that   send   and not

20 But the LORD hardened Pharaoh's heart, so that he would not let the children of Israel go.

פ

וַיֹּאמֶר יְהוָה אֶל־מֹשֶׁה נְטֵה יָדְךָ עַל־הַשָּׁמַיִם
    the heavens – upon   your hand   stretch   Moses - unto   ihvh   and he said

וִיהִי חֹשֶׁךְ עַל־אֶרֶץ מִצְרַיִם וְיָמֵשׁ חֹשֶׁךְ:
    darkness   and it grope   Egypt   land – upon   darkness   and there will be

21 And the LORD said unto Moses, Stretch out thine hand toward heaven, that there may be darkness over the land of Egypt, even darkness which may be felt.

וַיֵּט מֹשֶׁה אֶת־יָדוֹ עַל־הַשָּׁמָיִם
    the heavens – upon   his hand - that   Moses   and he stretched

וַיְהִי חֹשֶׁךְ־אֲפֵלָה בְּכָל־אֶרֶץ מִצְרַיִם שְׁלֹשֶׁת יָמִים:
    days   three   Egypt   land – in all   thick – darkness   and it was

22 And Moses stretched forth his hand toward heaven; and there was a thick darkness in all the land of Egypt three days:

לֹא־רָאוּ אִישׁ אֶת־אָחִיו
    his brother – that   man   they saw - not

וְלֹא־קָמוּ אִישׁ מִתַּחְתָּיו שְׁלֹשֶׁת יָמִים
    days   three   from his place   man   they rose – and not

וּלְכָל־בְּנֵי יִשְׂרָאֵל הָיָה אוֹר בְּמוֹשְׁבֹתָם:
    in their dwellings   light   was   Israel   sons - and to all

23 They saw not one another, neither rose any from his place for three days: but all the children of Israel had light in their dwellings.

[שלישי]

וַיִּקְרָא פַרְעֹה אֶל־מֹשֶׁה
    Moses - unto   Pharaoh   and he called

וַיִּקְרָא פַרְעֹה אֶל־מֹשֶׁה וַיֹּאמֶר לְכוּ עִבְדוּ אֶת־יְהוָה

ihvh – that   your serve   you go   and he said

רַק צֹאנְכֶם וּבְקַרְכֶם יֻצָּג

it stays   and your cattle   your flock   only

גַּם־טַפְּכֶם יֵלֵךְ עִמָּכֶם׃

with you   go   your little ones – also

24 And Pharaoh called unto Moses, and said, Go ye, serve the LORD; only let your flocks and your herds be stayed: let your little ones also go with you.

וַיֹּאמֶר מֹשֶׁה גַּם־אַתָּה תִּתֵּן בְּיָדֵנוּ זְבָחִים וְעֹלֹת

and offerings   sacrifices   in our hand   give   you – also   Moses   and he said

וְעָשִׂינוּ לַיהוָה אֱלֹהֵינוּ׃

our Elohim   to ihvh   and we do

25 And Moses said, Thou must give us also sacrifices and burnt offerings, that we may sacrifice unto the LORD our God.

וְגַם־מִקְנֵנוּ יֵלֵךְ עִמָּנוּ לֹא תִשָּׁאֵר פַּרְסָה

hoof   it remain   not   with us   it goes   our cattle – and also

כִּי מִמֶּנּוּ נִקַּח לַעֲבֹד אֶת־יְהוָה אֱלֹהֵינוּ

our Elohim   ihvh – that   to serve   we take   from us   like

וַאֲנַחְנוּ לֹא־נֵדַע מַה־נַּעֲבֹד אֶת־יְהוָה עַד־בֹּאֵנוּ שָׁמָּה׃

to there   we come – till   ihvh – that   we serve – what   we know – not   and we

26 Our cattle also shall go with us; there shall not an hoof be left behind; for thereof must we take to serve the LORD our God; and we know not with what we must serve the LORD, until we come thither.

וַיְחַזֵּק יְהוָה אֶת־לֵב פַּרְעֹה וְלֹא אָבָה לְשַׁלְּחָם׃

to send them   he complied   and not   Pharaoh   heart – that   ihvh   and he hardened

27 But the LORD hardened Pharaoh's heart, and he would not let them go.

וַיֹּאמֶר־לוֹ פַרְעֹה לֵךְ מֵעָלָי הִשָּׁמֶר לְךָ

you   caused to heed   from upon me   go   Pharaoh   to him – and he said

אַל־תֹּסֶף רְאוֹת פָּנַי

my face   seeing   you again - don't

כִּי בְּיוֹם רְאֹתְךָ פָנַי תָּמוּת׃

you will die   my face   you see   in day   like

28 And Pharaoh said unto him, Get thee from me, take heed to thyself, see my face no more; for in that day thou seest my face thou shalt die.

וַיֹּאמֶר מֹשֶׁה כֵּן דִּבַּרְתָּ לֹא־אֹסִף עוֹד רְאוֹת פָּנֶיךָ׃

your face   seeing   again   I continue – not   you spoke   thus   Moses   and he said

29 And Moses said, Thou hast spoken well, I will see thy face again no more.

CHAPTER 11

ספר שמות פרק יא

וַיֹּאמֶר יְהוָה אֶל־מֹשֶׁה
Moses – unto   ihvh   and he said

עוֹד נֶגַע אֶחָד אָבִיא עַל־פַּרְעֹה וְעַל־מִצְרַיִם
Egypt – and upon   Pharaoh – upon   I will bring   one   plague   still

אַחֲרֵי־כֵן יְשַׁלַּח אֶתְכֶם מִזֶּה
from this   that you   he will send   thus – after

כְּשַׁלְּחוֹ כָּלָה גָּרֵשׁ יְגָרֵשׁ אֶתְכֶם מִזֶּה׃
from this   that you   he will thrust   thrust   to all   like his sending

1 And the LORD said unto Moses, Yet will I bring one plague more upon Pharaoh, and upon Egypt; afterwards he will let you go hence: when he shall let you go, he shall surely thrust you out hence altogether.

דַּבֶּר־נָא בְּאָזְנֵי הָעָם וְיִשְׁאֲלוּ אִישׁ מֵאֵת רֵעֵהוּ
his neighbor   from that   man   and they ask   the people   in ears   now – speak

וְאִשָּׁה מֵאֵת רְעוּתָהּ כְּלֵי־כֶסֶף וּכְלֵי זָהָב׃
gold   and articles   silver – articles   her neighbor   from that   and woman

2 Speak now in the ears of the people, and let every man borrow of his neighbour, and every woman of her neighbour, jewels of silver, and jewels of gold.

וַיִּתֵּן יְהוָה אֶת־חֵן הָעָם בְּעֵינֵי מִצְרָיִם
Egyptians   in eyes   the people   grace – that   ihvh   and he gave

גַּם הָאִישׁ מֹשֶׁה גָּדוֹל מְאֹד בְּאֶרֶץ מִצְרַיִם
Egypt   in land   very   great   Moses   the man   also

בְּעֵינֵי עַבְדֵי־פַרְעֹה וּבְעֵינֵי הָעָם׃
the people   and in eyes   Pharaoh – servants   in eyes

3 And the LORD gave the people favour in the sight of the Egyptians. Moreover the man Moses was very great in the land of Egypt, in the sight of Pharaoh's servants, and in the sight of the people.

ס
[רביעי]

וַיֹּאמֶר מֹשֶׁה כֹּה אָמַר יְהוָה
ihvh   says   thus   Moses   and he said

כַּחֲצֹת הַלַּיְלָה אֲנִי יוֹצֵא בְּתוֹךְ מִצְרָיִם׃
Egypt   among   go out   I   the night   like mid

4 And Moses said, Thus saith the LORD, About midnight will I go out into

the midst of Egypt:

וּמֵת כָּל־בְּכוֹר בְּאֶרֶץ מִצְרַיִם

and die   first born – all   in land   Egypt

מִבְּכוֹר פַּרְעֹה הַיֹּשֵׁב עַל־כִּסְאוֹ

from first born   Pharaoh   the sitter   upon – his throne

עַד בְּכוֹר הַשִּׁפְחָה אֲשֶׁר אַחַר הָרֵחָיִם

till   first born   the maid servant   which   behind   the millstones

וְכֹל בְּכוֹר בְּהֵמָה׃

and all   first born   beasts

5 And all the firstborn in the land of Egypt shall die, from the firstborn of Pharaoh that sitteth upon his throne, even unto the firstborn of the maidservant that is behind the mill; and all the firstborn of beasts.

וְהָיְתָה צְעָקָה גְדֹלָה בְּכָל־אֶרֶץ מִצְרָיִם

and there will be   cry   great   in all – land   Egypt

אֲשֶׁר כָּמֹהוּ לֹא נִהְיָתָה וְכָמֹהוּ לֹא תֹסִף׃

which   like it   not   it has been   and like it   not   it again

6 And there shall be a great cry throughout all the land of Egypt, such as there was none like it, nor shall be like it any more.

וּלְכֹל בְּנֵי יִשְׂרָאֵל לֹא יֶחֱרַץ־כֶּלֶב לְשֹׁנוֹ

and to all   sons   Israel   not   dog – will point   to his tongue

לְמֵאִישׁ וְעַד־בְּהֵמָה

to from man   beast – and till

לְמַעַן תֵּדְעוּן אֲשֶׁר יַפְלֶה יְהוָה בֵּין מִצְרַיִם וּבֵין יִשְׂרָאֵל׃

to end   you will know   which   difference   ihvh   between   Egypt   and between   Israel

7 But against any of the children of Israel shall not a dog move his tongue, against man or beast: that ye may know how that the LORD doth put a difference between the Egyptians and Israel.

וְיָרְדוּ כָל־עֲבָדֶיךָ אֵלֶּה אֵלַי וְהִשְׁתַּחֲווּ־לִי לֵאמֹר

and they will descend   your servants – all   these   unto me   to me – they will bow   to say

צֵא אַתָּה וְכָל־הָעָם אֲשֶׁר־בְּרַגְלֶיךָ

go out   you   the people – and all   which – in your feet

וְאַחֲרֵי־כֵן אֵצֵא וַיֵּצֵא מֵעִם־פַּרְעֹה בָּחֳרִי־אָף׃

after – thus   I go will out   and he will go out   Pharaoh – from with   in kindled – anger

8 And all these thy servants shall come down unto me, and bow down themselves unto me, saying, Get thee out, and all the people that follow thee: and after that I will go out. And he went out from Pharaoh in a great anger.

ס

PARASHAT 3 - CHAPTER 11

וַיֹּ֤אמֶר יְהוָה֙ אֶל־מֹשֶׁ֔ה לֹא־יִשְׁמַ֥ע אֲלֵיכֶ֖ם פַּרְעֹ֑ה
Pharaoh   unto you   he will hear – not   Moses – unto   ihvh   and he said

לְמַ֛עַן רְב֥וֹת מוֹפְתַ֖י בְּאֶ֥רֶץ מִצְרָֽיִם׃
Egypt   in land   my wonders   many   to end

9 And the LORD said unto Moses, Pharaoh shall not hearken unto you; that my wonders may be multiplied in the land of Egypt.

וּמֹשֶׁ֣ה וְאַהֲרֹ֗ן עָשׂ֛וּ אֶת־כָּל־הַמֹּפְתִ֥ים הָאֵ֖לֶּה לִפְנֵ֣י פַרְעֹ֑ה
Pharaoh   before   the these   the wonders – all – that   they did   and Aaron   and Moses

וַיְחַזֵּ֤ק יְהוָה֙ אֶת־לֵ֣ב פַּרְעֹ֔ה
Pharaoh   heart – that   ihvh   and he hardened

וְלֹֽא־שִׁלַּ֥ח אֶת־בְּנֵֽי־יִשְׂרָאֵ֖ל מֵאַרְצֽוֹ׃
from his land   Israel – sons – that   send – and not

10 And Moses and Aaron did all these wonders before Pharaoh: and the LORD hardened Pharaoh's heart, so that he would not let the children of Israel go out of his land.

ס

Chapter 12

ספר שמות פרק יב

וַיֹּ֤אמֶר יְהוָה֙ אֶל־מֹשֶׁ֣ה וְאֶֽל־אַהֲרֹ֔ן בְּאֶ֥רֶץ מִצְרַ֖יִם לֵאמֹֽר׃
to say   Egypt   in land   Aaron – and unto   Moses – unto   ihvh   and he said

1 And the LORD spake unto Moses and Aaron in the land of Egypt, saying,

הַחֹ֧דֶשׁ הַזֶּ֛ה לָכֶ֖ם רֹ֣אשׁ חֳדָשִׁ֑ים
months   beginning   to you   the this   the month

רִאשׁ֥וֹן הוּא֙ לָכֶ֔ם לְחָדְשֵׁ֖י הַשָּׁנָֽה׃
the year   to months   to you   it   first

2 This month shall be unto you the beginning of months: it shall be the first month of the year to you.

דַּבְּר֗וּ אֶֽל־כָּל־עֲדַ֤ת יִשְׂרָאֵל֙ לֵאמֹ֔ר בֶּעָשֹׂ֖ר לַחֹ֣דֶשׁ הַזֶּ֑ה
the this   to month   in tenth   to say   Israel   congregation – all – unto   you speak

וְיִקְח֣וּ לָהֶ֗ם אִ֛ישׁ שֶׂ֥ה לְבֵית־אָבֹ֖ת שֶׂ֥ה לַבָּֽיִת׃
to house   lamb   fathers – to house   lamb   man   to them   and they will take

3 Speak ye unto all the congregation of Israel, saying, In the tenth day of this month they shall take to them every man a lamb, according to the house of their fathers, a lamb for an house:

וְאִם־יִמְעַ֣ט הַבַּ֘יִת֮ מִהְיֹ֣ת מִשֶּׂה֒
from lamb   from it being   the house   he little – and with

וְלָקַח הוּא וּשְׁכֵנוֹ הַקָּרֹב אֶל־בֵּיתוֹ בְּמִכְסַת נְפָשֹׁת
souls   in assesment   his house – unto   the close   and his dweller   it   and take

אִישׁ לְפִי אָכְלוֹ תָּכֹסּוּ עַל־הַשֶּׂה:
the lamb – upon   you assess it   his eat   to mouth   man

4 And if the household be too little for the lamb, let him and his neighbour next unto his house take it according to the number of the souls; every man according to his eating shall make your count for the lamb.

שֶׂה תָמִים זָכָר בֶּן־שָׁנָה יִהְיֶה לָכֶם
to them   it be   year – age   male   perfect   lamb

מִן־הַכְּבָשִׂים וּמִן־הָעִזִּים תִּקָּחוּ:
you take it   the goats – and from   the he lambs - from

5 Your lamb shall be without blemish, a male of the first year: ye shall take it out from the sheep, or from the goats:

וְהָיָה לָכֶם לְמִשְׁמֶרֶת עַד אַרְבָּעָה עָשָׂר יוֹם לַחֹדֶשׁ הַזֶּה
the this   to month   day   -- fourteen --   till   to duty   to them   and it be

וְשָׁחֲטוּ אֹתוֹ כֹּל קְהַל עֲדַת־יִשְׂרָאֵל בֵּין הָעַרְבָּיִם:
the evenings   between   Israel – congregation   assembly   all   to it   and you slay

6 And ye shall keep it up until the fourteenth day of the same month: and the whole assembly of the congregation of Israel shall kill it in the evening.

וְלָקְחוּ מִן־הַדָּם וְנָתְנוּ עַל־שְׁתֵּי הַמְּזוּזֹת
the door posts   two – upon   and you give   the blood – from   and you take it

וְעַל־הַמַּשְׁקוֹף עַל הַבָּתִּים אֲשֶׁר־יֹאכְלוּ אֹתוֹ בָּהֶם:
in them   to it   they eat – which   the houses   upon   upper door post – upon

7 And they shall take of the blood, and strike it on the two side posts and on the upper door post of the houses, wherein they shall eat it.

וְאָכְלוּ אֶת־הַבָּשָׂר בַּלַּיְלָה הַזֶּה
the this   in night   the flesh – that   and you will eat

צְלִי־אֵשׁ וּמַצּוֹת עַל־מְרֹרִים יֹאכְלֻהוּ:
they will eat it   bitter herbs – upon   and unleavened bread   fire – roast

8 And they shall eat the flesh in that night, roast with fire, and unleavened bread; and with bitter herbs they shall eat it.

אַל־תֹּאכְלוּ מִמֶּנּוּ נָא וּבָשֵׁל מְבֻשָּׁל בַּמָּיִם
in water   soaked   and cooked   raw   from it   you eat it – don't

כִּי אִם־צְלִי־אֵשׁ רֹאשׁוֹ עַל־כְּרָעָיו וְעַל־קִרְבּוֹ:
his insides – and upon   his legs – upon   his head   fire – roast – with   like

9 Eat not of it raw, nor sodden at all with water, but roast with fire; his head with his legs, and with the purtenance thereof.

וְלֹא־תוֹתִירוּ מִמֶּנּוּ עַד־בֹּקֶר
morning – till   from it   you reserve - and not

וְהַנֹּתָר מִמֶּנּוּ עַד־בֹּקֶר בָּאֵשׁ תִּשְׂרֹפוּ׃
you will burn it   in fire   morning – till   from it   and the remainder

10 And ye shall let nothing of it remain until the morning; and that which remaineth of it until the morning ye shall burn with fire.

וְכָכָה תֹּאכְלוּ אֹתוֹ מָתְנֵיכֶם חֲגֻרִים
girded   your loins   to it   you will eat it   and thus

נַעֲלֵיכֶם בְּרַגְלֵיכֶם וּמַקֶּלְכֶם בְּיֶדְכֶם
in your hand   and your stick   in your feet   your sandels

וַאֲכַלְתֶּם אֹתוֹ בְּחִפָּזוֹן פֶּסַח הוּא לַיהוָה׃
to ihvh   it   passover   in nervous haste   to it   and you will eat

11 And thus shall ye eat it; with your loins girded, your shoes on your feet, and your staff in your hand; and ye shall eat it in haste: it is the LORD'S passover.

וְעָבַרְתִּי בְאֶרֶץ־מִצְרַיִם בַּלַּיְלָה הַזֶּה
the this   in night   Egypt – in land   and I will pass

וְהִכֵּיתִי כָל־בְּכוֹר בְּאֶרֶץ מִצְרַיִם מֵאָדָם וְעַד־בְּהֵמָה
beast - and till   from Adam   Egypt   in land   first born – all   and I will cause smite

וּבְכָל־אֱלֹהֵי מִצְרַיִם אֶעֱשֶׂה שְׁפָטִים אֲנִי יְהוָה׃
ihvh   I   judgments   I will do   Egypt   elohim - and in all

12 For I will pass through the land of Egypt this night, and will smite all the firstborn in the land of Egypt, both man and beast; and against all the gods of Egypt I will execute judgment: I am the LORD.

וְהָיָה הַדָּם לָכֶם לְאֹת עַל הַבָּתִּים אֲשֶׁר אַתֶּם שָׁם
there   you   which   the houses   upon   to sign   to you   the blood   and there will be

וְרָאִיתִי אֶת־הַדָּם וּפָסַחְתִּי עֲלֵכֶם
upon you   I will pass over   the blood – that   and I will see

וְלֹא־יִהְיֶה בָכֶם נֶגֶף לְמַשְׁחִית בְּהַכֹּתִי בְּאֶרֶץ מִצְרָיִם׃
Egypt   in land   in my smiting   to destroy   plague   in you   it will be – and not

13 And the blood shall be to you for a token upon the houses where ye are: and when I see the blood, I will pass over you, and the plague shall not be upon you to destroy you, when I smite the land of Egypt.

וְהָיָה הַיּוֹם הַזֶּה לָכֶם לְזִכָּרוֹן
to remembrance   to you   the this   the day   and it will be

וְחַגֹּתֶם אֹתוֹ חַג לַיהוָה לְדֹרֹתֵיכֶם חֻקַּת עוֹלָם תְּחָגֻּהוּ׃
you feast it   forever   statute   to your generations   to ihvh   festival   to it   and you festival

14 And this day shall be unto you for a memorial; and ye shall keep it a feast to

the LORD throughout your generations; ye shall keep it a feast by an ordinance for ever.

שִׁבְעַת יָמִים מַצּוֹת תֹּאכֵלוּ
seven days unleavened bread you will eat it

אַךְ בַּיּוֹם הָרִאשׁוֹן תַּשְׁבִּיתוּ שְּׂאֹר מִבָּתֵּיכֶם
certainly in day the first you will eradicate remainder from your houses

כִּי כָּל־אֹכֵל חָמֵץ וְנִכְרְתָה הַנֶּפֶשׁ הַהִוא מִיִּשְׂרָאֵל
like all – eater yeast and will be cut off the soul the it from Israel

מִיּוֹם הָרִאשֹׁן עַד־יוֹם הַשְּׁבִעִי:
from day the first till – day the seventh

15 Seven days shall ye eat unleavened bread; even the first day ye shall put away leaven out of your houses: for whosoever eateth leavened bread from the first day until the seventh day, that soul shall be cut off from Israel.

וּבַיּוֹם הָרִאשׁוֹן מִקְרָא־קֹדֶשׁ
and in day the first holy – meeting

וּבַיּוֹם הַשְּׁבִיעִי מִקְרָא־קֹדֶשׁ יִהְיֶה לָכֶם
and in day the seventh holy – meeting it will be to you

כָּל־מְלָאכָה לֹא־יֵעָשֶׂה בָהֶם
all - work not - he will do in them

אַךְ אֲשֶׁר יֵאָכֵל לְכָל־נֶפֶשׁ הוּא לְבַדּוֹ יֵעָשֶׂה לָכֶם:
only which he will eat to all – soul it alone he will do to you

16 And in the first day there shall be an holy convocation, and in the seventh day there shall be an holy convocation to you; no manner of work shall be done in them, save that which every man must eat, that only may be done of you.

וּשְׁמַרְתֶּם אֶת־הַמַּצּוֹת כִּי בְּעֶצֶם הַיּוֹם הַזֶּה
and you will heed the unleavened bread – that like in exactly the day the this

הוֹצֵאתִי אֶת־צִבְאוֹתֵיכֶם מֵאֶרֶץ מִצְרָיִם
I brought out that – your armies from land Egypt

וּשְׁמַרְתֶּם אֶת־הַיּוֹם הַזֶּה לְדֹרֹתֵיכֶם חֻקַּת עוֹלָם:
and you will heed that – the day the this to your generations statute forever

17 And ye shall observe the feast of unleavened bread; for in this selfsame day have I brought your armies out of the land of Egypt: therefore shall ye observe this day in your generations by an ordinance for ever.

בָּרִאשֹׁן בְּאַרְבָּעָה עָשָׂר יוֹם לַחֹדֶשׁ בָּעֶרֶב
in first -- in fourteen -- day to month in evening

תֹּאכְלוּ מַצֹּת עַד יוֹם הָאֶחָד וְעֶשְׂרִים לַחֹדֶשׁ בָּעָרֶב:
you will eat unleavened bread till day the one and twentieth to month in evening

18 In the first month, on the fourteenth day of the month at even, ye shall eat unleavened bread, until the one and twentieth day of the month at even.

שִׁבְעַת יָמִים שְׂאֹר לֹא יִמָּצֵא בְּבָתֵּיכֶם
seven days leaven not it be found in your houses

כִּי כָּל־אֹכֵל מַחְמֶצֶת
like all – eater leavened bread

וְנִכְרְתָה הַנֶּפֶשׁ הַהִוא מֵעֲדַת יִשְׂרָאֵל
and will be cut off the soul the it from congregation Israel

בַּגֵּר וּבְאֶזְרַח הָאָרֶץ:
in stranger and in native born the land

19 Seven days shall there be no leaven found in your houses: for whosoever eateth that which is leavened, even that soul shall be cut off from the congregation of Israel, whether he be a stranger, or born in the land.

כָּל־מַחְמֶצֶת לֹא תֹאכֵלוּ בְּכֹל מוֹשְׁבֹתֵיכֶם תֹּאכְלוּ מַצּוֹת:
all – leaven bread not you will eat it in all your habitations you will eat it unleavened

20 Ye shall eat nothing leavened; in all your habitations shall ye eat unleavened bread.

פ
[חמישי]

וַיִּקְרָא מֹשֶׁה לְכָל־זִקְנֵי יִשְׂרָאֵל
and he called Moses elders – to all Israel

וַיֹּאמֶר אֲלֵהֶם מִשְׁכוּ וּקְחוּ לָכֶם צֹאן לְמִשְׁפְּחֹתֵיכֶם
and he said unto them you draw out and you take to you lamb to your families

וְשַׁחֲטוּ הַפָּסַח:
and slay it the passover

21 Then Moses called for all the elders of Israel, and said unto them, Draw out and take you a lamb according to your families, and kill the passover.

וּלְקַחְתֶּם אֲגֻדַּת אֵזוֹב
and you take bunch hyssop

וּטְבַלְתֶּם בַּדָּם אֲשֶׁר־בַּסַּף וְהִגַּעְתֶּם אֶל־הַמַּשְׁקוֹף
and dip them in blood which – in basin and you touch unto – the lintel

וְאֶל־שְׁתֵּי הַמְּזוּזֹת מִן־הַדָּם אֲשֶׁר בַּסָּף
and unto – two the door posts from – blood which in basin

וְאַתֶּם לֹא תֵצְאוּ אִישׁ מִפֶּתַח־בֵּיתוֹ עַד־בֹּקֶר:
and you not you will go out man from opening – his house till – morning

22 And ye shall take a bunch of hyssop, and dip it in the blood that is in the basin, and strike the lintel and the two side posts with the blood that is in the basin; and none of you shall go out at the door of his house until the morning.

וְעָבַר יְהוָה לִנְגֹּף אֶת־מִצְרַיִם
and will pass ihvh to strike that – Egyptians

וְרָאָה אֶת־הַדָּם עַל־הַמַּשְׁקוֹף וְעַל שְׁתֵּי הַמְּזוּזֹת
and see the blood – that lintel – upon and upon two the door posts

וּפָסַח יְהוָה עַל־הַפֶּתַח
and will pass over ihvh the opening - upon

וְלֹא יִתֵּן הַמַּשְׁחִית לָבֹא אֶל־בָּתֵּיכֶם לִנְגֹּף׃
and not he will give the destroyer to come unto – your houses to strike

23 For the LORD will pass through to smite the Egyptians; and when he seeth the blood upon the lintel, and on the two side posts, the LORD will pass over the door, and will not suffer the destroyer to come in unto your houses to smite you.

וּשְׁמַרְתֶּם אֶת־הַדָּבָר הַזֶּה לְחָק־לְךָ וּלְבָנֶיךָ עַד־עוֹלָם׃
and you will heed that – the matter the this to statute – you to your sons till – ever

24 And ye shall observe this thing for an ordinance to thee and to thy sons for ever.

וְהָיָה כִּי־תָבֹאוּ אֶל־הָאָרֶץ
and it will be like – you will come it unto - the land

אֲשֶׁר יִתֵּן יְהוָה לָכֶם כַּאֲשֶׁר דִּבֵּר
which he gives ihvh to you when spoke

וּשְׁמַרְתֶּם אֶת־הָעֲבֹדָה הַזֹּאת׃
and you will heed that – the service the this

25 And it shall come to pass, when ye be come to the land which the LORD will give you, according as he hath promised, that ye shall keep this service.

וְהָיָה כִּי־יֹאמְרוּ אֲלֵיכֶם בְּנֵיכֶם מָה הָעֲבֹדָה הַזֹּאת לָכֶם׃
and it be like – they will say unto you your sons what the service the this to you

26 And it shall come to pass, when your children shall say unto you, What mean ye by this service?

וַאֲמַרְתֶּם זֶבַח־פֶּסַח הוּא לַיהוָה
and you will say sacrifice – passover it to ihvh

אֲשֶׁר פָּסַח עַל־בָּתֵּי בְנֵי־יִשְׂרָאֵל בְּמִצְרַיִם
which pass over upon – houses sons – Israel in Egypt

בְּנָגְפּוֹ אֶת־מִצְרַיִם
in his striking that – Egyptians

PARASHAT 3 - CHAPTER 12   89

וְאֶת־בָּתֵּינוּ הִצִּיל
resued　our houses – and that

וַיִּקֹּד הָעָם וַיִּשְׁתַּחֲוּוּ׃
and they bowed down　the people　and he bowed head

27 That ye shall say, It is the sacrifice of the LORD'S passover, who passed over the houses of the children of Israel in Egypt, when he smote the Egyptians, and delivered our houses. And the people bowed the head and worshipped.

וַיֵּלְכוּ וַיַּעֲשׂוּ בְּנֵי יִשְׂרָאֵל
Israel　sons　and they did　and they went

כַּאֲשֶׁר צִוָּה יְהוָה אֶת־מֹשֶׁה וְאַהֲרֹן כֵּן עָשׂוּ׃
they did　thus　and Aaron　Moses – that　ihvh　commanded　when

28 And the children of Israel went away, and did as the LORD had commanded Moses and Aaron, so did they.

ס
[ששי]

וַיְהִי בַּחֲצִי הַלַּיְלָה
the night　in half　and it be

וַיהוָה הִכָּה כָל־בְּכוֹר בְּאֶרֶץ מִצְרַיִם
Egypt　in land　first born – all　smote　and ihvh

מִבְּכֹר פַּרְעֹה הַיֹּשֵׁב עַל־כִּסְאוֹ
his throne – upon　the sitter　Pharaoh　from first born

עַד בְּכוֹר הַשְּׁבִי אֲשֶׁר בְּבֵית הַבּוֹר
the dungeon　in house　which　the captive　first born　till

וְכֹל בְּכוֹר בְּהֵמָה׃
cattle　first born　and all

29 And it came to pass, that at midnight the LORD smote all the firstborn in the land of Egypt, from the firstborn of Pharaoh that sat on his throne unto the firstborn of the captive that was in the dungeon; and all the firstborn of cattle.

וַיָּקָם פַּרְעֹה לַיְלָה הוּא וְכָל־עֲבָדָיו וְכָל־מִצְרַיִם
Egyptians – and all　his servants – and all　he　night　Pharaoh　and he rose

וַתְּהִי צְעָקָה גְדֹלָה בְּמִצְרָיִם
in Egypt　great　cry　and it was

כִּי־אֵין בַּיִת אֲשֶׁר אֵין־שָׁם מֵת׃
death　these – isn't　which　house　isn't – like

30 And Pharaoh rose up in the night, he, and all his servants, and all the Egyp-

tians; and there was a great cry in Egypt; for there was not a house where there was not one dead.

וַיִּקְרָא לְמֹשֶׁה וּלְאַהֲרֹן לַיְלָה
and he called   to Moses   and to Aaron   night

וַיֹּאמֶר קוּמוּ צְּאוּ מִתּוֹךְ עַמִּי גַּם־אַתֶּם גַּם־בְּנֵי יִשְׂרָאֵל
and he said   you rise   you go out   from midst   my people   also – you   also – sons   Israel

וּלְכוּ עִבְדוּ אֶת־יְהֹוָה כְּדַבֶּרְכֶם׃
and you go   you serve   ihvh – that   like you spoke

31 And he called for Moses and Aaron by night, and said, Rise up, and get you forth from among my people, both ye and the children of Israel; and go, serve the LORD, as ye have said.

גַּם־צֹאנְכֶם גַּם־בְּקַרְכֶם קְחוּ כַּאֲשֶׁר דִּבַּרְתֶּם
also – your sheep   also – your herds   you take   when   you spoke

וָלֵכוּ וּבֵרַכְתֶּם גַּם־אֹתִי׃
and you go   and you bless   also – to me

32 Also take your flocks and your herds, as ye have said, and be gone; and bless me also.

וַתֶּחֱזַק מִצְרַיִם עַל־הָעָם לְמַהֵר לְשַׁלְּחָם מִן־הָאָרֶץ
and it forced   Egyptians   upon – the people   to hurry   to send them   from – the land

כִּי אָמְרוּ כֻּלָּנוּ מֵתִים׃
like   they said   all us   dead ones

33 And the Egyptians were urgent upon the people, that they might send them out of the land in haste; for they said, We be all dead men.

וַיִּשָּׂא הָעָם אֶת־בְּצֵקוֹ טֶרֶם יֶחְמָץ מִשְׁאֲרֹתָם צְרֻרֹת
and he lifted   the people   his dough – that   before   it leavened   from their kneading   troughs

בְּשִׂמְלֹתָם עַל־שִׁכְמָם׃
in their garment   upon – their shoulders

34 And the people took their dough before it was leavened, their kneading troughs being bound up in their clothes upon their shoulders.

וּבְנֵי־יִשְׂרָאֵל עָשׂוּ כִּדְבַר מֹשֶׁה
and sons – Israel   they did   like spoke   Moses

וַיִּשְׁאֲלוּ מִמִּצְרַיִם כְּלֵי־כֶסֶף וּכְלֵי זָהָב וּשְׂמָלֹת׃
and they asked   from Egyptians   articles – silver   and articles   gold   and garments

35 And the children of Israel did according to the word of Moses; and they borrowed of the Egyptians jewels of silver, and jewels of gold, and raiment:

וַיהוָה נָתַן אֶת־חֵן הָעָם בְּעֵינֵי מִצְרַיִם
and ihvh   gave   that – grace   the people   in eyes   Egypt

וַיִּשְׁאָלוּם וַיְנַצְּלוּ אֶת־מִצְרָיִם׃
Egyptians – that   and they despoiled   and they asked them

36 And the LORD gave the people favour in the sight of the Egyptians, so that they lent unto them such things as they required. And they spoiled the Egyptians.

פ

וַיִּסְעוּ בְנֵי־יִשְׂרָאֵל
Israel – sons   and they journeyed

מֵרַעְמְסֵס סֻכֹּתָה כְּשֵׁשׁ־מֵאוֹת אֶלֶף רַגְלִי הַגְּבָרִים
the mighty men feet thousand hundred - like six toward Succoth from Rameses

לְבַד מִטָּף׃
small tots   besides

37 And the children of Israel journeyed from Rameses to Succoth, about six hundred thousand on foot that were men, beside children.

וְגַם־עֵרֶב רַב עָלָה אִתָּם
with them went up much mixed multitude - also

וְצֹאן וּבָקָר מִקְנֶה כָּבֵד מְאֹד׃
very heavy cattle and herds and sheep

38 And a mixed multitude went up also with them; and flocks, and herds, even very much cattle.

וַיֹּאפוּ אֶת־הַבָּצֵק אֲשֶׁר הוֹצִיאוּ מִמִּצְרַיִם עֻגֹת מַצּוֹת
unleavened cakes from Egypt they took out which dough – that and they baked

כִּי לֹא חָמֵץ כִּי־גֹרְשׁוּ מִמִּצְרַיִם
from Egypt they driven out – like leavened not like

וְלֹא יָכְלוּ לְהִתְמַהְמֵהַּ וְגַם־צֵדָה לֹא־עָשׂוּ לָהֶם׃
to them they did – not provision – and also to tarry it they able and not

39 And they baked unleavened cakes of the dough which they brought forth out of Egypt, for it was not leavened; because they were thrust out of Egypt, and could not tarry, neither had they prepared for themselves any victual.

וּמוֹשַׁב בְּנֵי יִשְׂרָאֵל אֲשֶׁר יָשְׁבוּ בְּמִצְרָיִם
in Egypt they dwelt which Israel sons and dwelling

שְׁלֹשִׁים שָׁנָה וְאַרְבַּע מֵאוֹת שָׁנָה׃
year hundred and four year thirty

40 Now the sojourning of the children of Israel, who dwelt in Egypt, was four hundred and thirty years.

וַיְהִי מִקֵּץ שְׁלֹשִׁים שָׁנָה וְאַרְבַּע מֵאוֹת שָׁנָה
year hundred and four year thirty from end and it was

וַיְהִ֗י בְּעֶ֙צֶם֙ הַיּ֣וֹם הַזֶּ֔ה
the this   the day   in exactly   and it was

יָ֥צְא֛וּ כָּל־צִבְא֥וֹת יְהוָ֖ה מֵאֶ֥רֶץ מִצְרָֽיִם׃
Egypt   from land   ihvh   hosts–all   they went out

41 And it came to pass at the end of the four hundred and thirty years, even the selfsame day it came to pass, that all the hosts of the LORD went out from the land of Egypt.

לֵ֣יל שִׁמֻּרִ֥ים ה֛וּא לַֽיהוָ֖ה
to ihvh   it   heeding ones   night

לְהוֹצִיאָ֖ם מֵאֶ֣רֶץ מִצְרָ֑יִם הֽוּא־הַלַּ֤יְלָה הַזֶּה֙ לַֽיהוָ֔ה
to ihvh   the this   the night–it   Egypt   from land   to bringing them out

שִׁמֻּרִ֛ים לְכָל־בְּנֵ֥י יִשְׂרָאֵ֖ל לְדֹרֹתָֽם׃
to their generations   Israel   sons–to all   heeding ones

42 It is a night to be much observed unto the LORD for bringing them out from the land of Egypt: this is that night of the LORD to be observed of all the children of Israel in their generations.

פ

וַיֹּ֤אמֶר יְהוָה֙ אֶל־מֹשֶׁ֣ה וְאַהֲרֹ֔ן
and Aaron   Moses–unto   ihvh   and he said

זֹ֖את חֻקַּ֣ת הַפָּ֑סַח כָּל־בֶּן־נֵכָ֖ר לֹא־יֹ֥אכַל בּֽוֹ׃
in it   he will eat–not   stranger–from–all   the Passover   statute   this

43 And the LORD said unto Moses and Aaron, This is the ordinance of the passover: There shall no stranger eat thereof:

וְכָל־עֶ֥בֶד אִ֖ישׁ מִקְנַת־כָּ֑סֶף וּמַלְתָּ֣ה אֹת֔וֹ אָ֖ז יֹ֥אכַל בּֽוֹ׃
in it   he will eat   then   to him   and it circumcised   money–from bought   man   servant–and all

44 But every man's servant that is bought for money, when thou hast circumcised him, then shall he eat thereof.

תּוֹשָׁ֥ב וְשָׂכִ֖יר לֹא־יֹ֥אכַל בּֽוֹ׃
in it   he eat–not   hired servant   it dweller (guest)

45 A foreigner and an hired servant shall not eat thereof.

בְּבַ֤יִת אֶחָד֙ יֵֽאָכֵ֔ל לֹא־תוֹצִ֧יא מִן־הַבַּ֛יִת מִן־הַבָּשָׂ֖ר ח֑וּצָה
outside   the flesh–from   the house–from   it go out–not   he eats   one   in house

וְעֶ֖צֶם לֹ֥א תִשְׁבְּרוּ־בֽוֹ׃
in it–you break it   not   and exactly

46 In one house shall it be eaten; thou shalt not carry forth ought of the flesh abroad out of the house; neither shall ye break a bone thereof.

$$\text{כָּל־עֲדַת יִשְׂרָאֵל יַעֲשׂוּ אֹתוֹ:}$$
to it   they will do   Israel   congregation – all

47 All the congregation of Israel shall keep it.

$$\text{וְכִי־יָגוּר אִתְּךָ גֵּר}$$
stranger   with you   he sojourn – and like

$$\text{וְעָשָׂה פֶסַח לַיהוָה הִמּוֹל לוֹ כָל־זָכָר}$$
males – all   to him   circumcised   to ihvh   pass over   and will do

$$\text{וְאָז יִקְרַב לַעֲשֹׂתוֹ וְהָיָה כְּאֶזְרַח הָאָרֶץ}$$
the land   like one born   and it will be   to his doers   he near   and then

$$\text{וְכָל־עָרֵל לֹא־יֹאכַל בּוֹ:}$$
in it   he will eat – not   uncircumcised – and all

48 And when a stranger shall sojourn with thee, and will keep the passover to the LORD, let all his males be circumcised, and then let him come near and keep it; and he shall be as one that is born in the land: for no uncircumcised person shall eat thereof.

$$\text{תּוֹרָה אַחַת יִהְיֶה לָאֶזְרָח וְלַגֵּר הַגָּר בְּתוֹכְכֶם:}$$
in your midst   the living   and to stranger   to native born   it will be   one   law

49 One law shall be to him that is homeborn, and unto the stranger that sojourneth among you.

$$\text{וַיַּעֲשׂוּ כָּל־בְּנֵי יִשְׂרָאֵל}$$
Israel   sons – all   and they did

$$\text{כַּאֲשֶׁר צִוָּה יְהוָה אֶת־מֹשֶׁה וְאֶת־אַהֲרֹן כֵּן עָשׂוּ:}$$
they did   thus   Aaron – and that   Moses – that   ihvh   commanded   when

50 Thus did all the children of Israel; as the LORD commanded Moses and Aaron, so did they.

ס

$$\text{וַיְהִי בְּעֶצֶם הַיּוֹם הַזֶּה}$$
the this   the day   in exactly   and it was

$$\text{הוֹצִיא יְהוָה אֶת־בְּנֵי יִשְׂרָאֵל מֵאֶרֶץ מִצְרַיִם עַל־צִבְאֹתָם:}$$
their armies – upon   Egypt   from land   Israel   sons – that   ihvh   bringer out

51 And it came to pass the selfsame day, that the LORD did bring the children of Israel out of the land of Egypt by their armies.

פ

Chapter 13

ספר שמות פרק יג
[שביעי]

וַיְדַבֵּר יְהֹוָה אֶל־מֹשֶׁה לֵּאמֹר:
to say Moses – unto ihvh and he spoke

1 And the LORD spake unto Moses, saying,

קַדֶּשׁ־לִי כָל־בְּכוֹר פֶּטֶר כָּל־רֶחֶם בִּבְנֵי יִשְׂרָאֵל
Israel in sons womb – all openeth first born – all to me – sanctify

בָּאָדָם וּבַבְּהֵמָה לִי הוּא:
it to me and in beasts in Adam

2 Sanctify unto me all the firstborn, whatsoever openeth the womb among the children of Israel, both of man and of beast: it is mine.

וַיֹּאמֶר מֹשֶׁה אֶל־הָעָם זָכוֹר אֶת־הַיּוֹם הַזֶּה
the thus the day – that remember the people – unto Moses and he said

אֲשֶׁר יְצָאתֶם מִמִּצְרַיִם מִבֵּית עֲבָדִים
slaves from house from Egypt you came out which

כִּי בְּחֹזֶק יָד הוֹצִיא יְהֹוָה אֶתְכֶם מִזֶּה
from this that you ihvh brought out hand in strength like

וְלֹא יֵאָכֵל חָמֵץ:
leaven it will be eaten and not

3 And Moses said unto the people, Remember this day, in which ye came out from Egypt, out of the house of bondage; for by strength of hand the LORD brought you out from this place: there shall no leavened bread be eaten.

הַיּוֹם אַתֶּם יֹצְאִים בְּחֹדֶשׁ הָאָבִיב:
the Aviv in month coming out ones you the day

4 This day came ye out in the month Abib.

וְהָיָה כִי־יְבִיאֲךָ יְהֹוָה אֶל־אֶרֶץ הַכְּנַעֲנִי
the Canaanites land – unto ihvh he brought you – like and it will be

וְהַחִתִּי וְהָאֱמֹרִי וְהַחִוִּי וְהַיְבוּסִי
and the Jebusites and the Hivites and the Amorites and the Hittites

אֲשֶׁר נִשְׁבַּע לַאֲבֹתֶיךָ לָתֶת לָךְ אֶרֶץ זָבַת חָלָב וּדְבָשׁ
and honey milk flowing land to you to give to your fathers swore which

וְעָבַדְתָּ אֶת־הָעֲבֹדָה הַזֹּאת בַּחֹדֶשׁ הַזֶּה:
the this in month the this the service – that and you will serve

5 And it shall be when the LORD shall bring thee into the land of the Canaanites, and the Hittites, and the Amorites, and the Hivites, and the Jebusites,

which he sware unto thy fathers to give thee, a land flowing with milk and honey, that thou shalt keep this service in this month.

שִׁבְעַת יָמִים תֹּאכַל מַצֹּת וּבַיּוֹם הַשְּׁבִיעִי חַג לַיהוָֹה:
seven   days   you will eat   unleavened   and in day   the seventh   festival   to ihvh

6 Seven days thou shalt eat unleavened bread, and in the seventh day shall be a feast to the LORD.

מַצּוֹת יֵאָכֵל אֵת שִׁבְעַת הַיָּמִים
unleavened   it will be eaten   that   seven   the days

וְלֹא־יֵרָאֶה לְךָ חָמֵץ וְלֹא־יֵרָאֶה לְךָ שְׂאֹר בְּכָל־גְּבֻלֶךָ:
and not – it will be seen   to you   leaven   and not – it will be seen   to you   yeast   in all – your borders

7 Unleavened bread shall be eaten seven days; and there shall no leavened bread be seen with thee, neither shall there be leaven seen with thee in all thy quarters.

וְהִגַּדְתָּ לְבִנְךָ בַּיּוֹם הַהוּא
and you will tell   to your sons   in day   the it

לֵאמֹר בַּעֲבוּר זֶה עָשָׂה יְהוָֹה לִי בְּצֵאתִי מִמִּצְרָיִם:
to say   in past   this   did   ihvh   to me   in my coming out   from Egypt

8 And thou shalt shew thy son in that day, saying, This is done because of that which the LORD did unto me when I came forth out of Egypt.

וְהָיָה לְךָ לְאוֹת עַל־יָדְךָ
and it was   to you   to sign   upon – your hand

וּלְזִכָּרוֹן בֵּין עֵינֶיךָ לְמַעַן תִּהְיֶה תּוֹרַת יְהוָֹה בְּפִיךָ
and to memorial   between   your eyes   to end   it will be   law   ihvh   in your mouth

כִּי בְּיָד חֲזָקָה הוֹצִאֲךָ יְהוָֹה מִמִּצְרָיִם:
like   in hand   strong   brought you out   ihvh   from Egypt

9 And it shall be for a sign unto thee upon thine hand, and for a memorial between thine eyes, that the LORD'S law may be in thy mouth: for with a strong hand hath the LORD brought thee out of Egypt.

וְשָׁמַרְתָּ אֶת־הַחֻקָּה הַזֹּאת לְמוֹעֲדָהּ מִיָּמִים יָמִימָה:
and you will heed   that – the statute   the this   to season   from years   to year

10 Thou shalt therefore keep this ordinance in his season from year to year.

פ

וְהָיָה כִּי־יְבִאֲךָ יְהוָֹה אֶל־אֶרֶץ הַכְּנַעֲנִי
and it will be   like – he will bring you   ihvh   unto – land   Canaanites

כַּאֲשֶׁר נִשְׁבַּע לְךָ וְלַאֲבֹתֶיךָ וּנְתָנָהּ לָךְ:
when   swore   to you   and to your fathers   and will give it   to you

11 And it shall be when the LORD shall bring thee into the land of the Ca-

PARASHAT 3 - CHAPTER 13

naanites, as he sware unto thee and to thy fathers, and shall give it thee,

וְהַעֲבַרְתָּ֛ כָּל־פֶּֽטֶר־רֶ֖חֶם לַֽיהֹוָ֑ה
and you will the pass — all - openeth - womb — to ihvh

וְכָל־פֶּ֣טֶר ׀ שֶׁ֣גֶר בְּהֵמָ֗ה אֲשֶׁ֨ר יִהְיֶ֥ה לְךָ֛ הַזְּכָרִ֖ים לַיהֹוָֽה׃
and all - openeth drop beast which it will be to you the male ones to ihvh

12 That thou shalt set apart unto the LORD all that openeth the matrix, and every firstling that cometh of a beast which thou hast; the males shall be the LORD'S.

וְכָל־פֶּ֤טֶר חֲמֹר֙ תִּפְדֶּ֣ה בְשֶׂ֔ה
and all - openeth ass you will redeem in lamb

וְאִם־לֹ֥א תִפְדֶּ֖ה וַעֲרַפְתּ֑וֹ
and with – not you redeem and break his neck

וְכֹ֨ל בְּכ֥וֹר אָדָ֛ם בְּבָנֶ֖יךָ תִּפְדֶּֽה׃
and all first born Adam in your sons you will redeem

13 And every firstling of an ass thou shalt redeem with a lamb; and if thou wilt not redeem it, then thou shalt break his neck: and all the firstborn of man among thy children shalt thou redeem.

[מפטיר]

וְהָיָ֞ה כִּֽי־יִשְׁאָלְךָ֥ בִנְךָ֛ מָחָ֖ר לֵאמֹ֣ר מַה־זֹּ֑את
and it will be like – he will ask you your son tomorrow to say what – this

וְאָמַרְתָּ֣ אֵלָ֔יו
and you will say unto him

בְּחֹ֣זֶק יָ֗ד הוֹצִיאָ֧נוּ יְהֹוָ֛ה מִמִּצְרַ֖יִם מִבֵּ֥ית עֲבָדִֽים׃
in strength hand brought us out ihvh from Egypt from house slavery

14 And it shall be when thy son asketh thee in time to come, saying, What is this? that thou shalt say unto him, By strength of hand the LORD brought us out from Egypt, from the house of bondage:

וַיְהִ֗י כִּֽי־הִקְשָׁ֣ה פַרְעֹה֮ לְשַׁלְּחֵנוּ֒
and it was like – hardened Pharaoh to send us

וַיַּהֲרֹ֨ג יְהֹוָ֤ה כָּל־בְּכוֹר֙ בְּאֶ֣רֶץ מִצְרַ֔יִם
and he slew ihvh all – first born in land Egyptian

מִבְּכֹ֥ר אָדָ֖ם וְעַד־בְּכ֣וֹר בְּהֵמָ֑ה
from first born Adam and till – first born beast

עַל־כֵּן֩ אֲנִ֨י זֹבֵ֜חַ לַיהֹוָ֗ה כָּל־פֶּ֤טֶר רֶ֙חֶם֙ הַזְּכָרִ֔ים
upon – thus I sacrifice to ihvh all – openeth womb the male ones

וְכָל־בְּכוֹר בָּנַי אֶפְדֶּה׃
I redeem   sons   first born – and all

15 And it came to pass, when Pharaoh would hardly let us go, that the LORD slew all the firstborn in the land of Egypt, both the firstborn of man, and the firstborn of beast: therefore I sacrifice to the LORD all that openeth the matrix, being males; but all the firstborn of my children I redeem.

וְהָיָה לְאוֹת עַל־יָדְכָה וּלְטוֹטָפֹת בֵּין עֵינֶיךָ
your eyes   between   and frontlets   your hand – upon   to sign   and it will be

כִּי בְּחֹזֶק יָד הוֹצִיאָנוּ יְהֹוָה מִמִּצְרָיִם׃
from Egypt   ihvh   brought us out   hand   in strong   like

16 And it shall be for a token upon thine hand, and for frontlets between thine eyes: for by strength of hand the LORD brought us forth out of Egypt.

ס ס ס

Parashat 4 - Beshalach

Chapter 13 cont

[פרשת בשלח]

וַיְהִ֗י בְּשַׁלַּ֣ח פַּרְעֹה֮ אֶת־הָעָם֒
and it was   in sending   Pharaoh   the people – that

וְלֹא־נָחָ֣ם אֱלֹהִ֗ים דֶּ֚רֶךְ אֶ֣רֶץ פְּלִשְׁתִּ֔ים כִּ֥י קָר֖וֹב ה֑וּא
led – and not   Elohim   way   land   Philistines   like   near   It

כִּ֣י ׀ אָמַ֣ר אֱלֹהִ֗ים פֶּֽן־יִנָּחֵ֥ם הָעָ֛ם בִּרְאֹתָ֥ם מִלְחָמָ֖ה
like   said   Elohim   lest – he lead   the people   in their sight   war

וְשָׁ֥בוּ מִצְרָֽיְמָה׃
and they return   towards Egypt

17 And it came to pass, when Pharaoh had let the people go, that God led them not through the way of the land of the Philistines, although that was near; for God said, Lest peradventure the people repent when they see war, and they return to Egypt:

וַיַּסֵּ֨ב אֱלֹהִ֧ים ׀ אֶת־הָעָ֛ם דֶּ֥רֶךְ הַמִּדְבָּ֖ר יַם־ס֑וּף
and he turned around   Elohim   the people – that   way   the wilderness   sea – end

וַחֲמֻשִׁ֛ים עָל֥וּ בְנֵי־יִשְׂרָאֵ֖ל מֵאֶ֥רֶץ מִצְרָֽיִם׃
and five parts   they went up   Israel – sons   from land   Egypt

18 But God led the people about, through the way of the wilderness of the Red sea: and the children of Israel went up harnessed out of the land of Egypt.

וַיִּקַּ֥ח מֹשֶׁ֛ה אֶת־עַצְמ֥וֹת יוֹסֵ֖ף עִמּ֑וֹ
and he took   Moses   bones – that   Joseph   with him

כִּי֩ הַשְׁבֵּ֨עַ הִשְׁבִּ֜יעַ אֶת־בְּנֵ֤י יִשְׂרָאֵל֙ לֵאמֹ֔ר
like   the swearing   caused swear   son – that   Israel   to say

פָּקֹ֨ד יִפְקֹ֤ד אֱלֹהִים֙ אֶתְכֶ֔ם
visit   he will visit   Elohim   that you

וְהַעֲלִיתֶ֧ם אֶת־עַצְמֹתַ֛י מִזֶּ֖ה אִתְּכֶֽם׃
and the ascend you   my bones – that   from this   with you

19 And Moses took the bones of Joseph with him: for he had straitly sworn the children of Israel, saying, God will surely visit you; and ye shall carry up my bones away hence with you.

וַיִּסְע֖וּ מִסֻּכֹּ֑ת וַיַּחֲנ֣וּ בְאֵתָ֔ם בִּקְצֵ֖ה הַמִּדְבָּֽר׃
and they journeyed   from Succoth   they tented   in Etham   in edge   the wilderness

20 And they took their journey from Succoth, and encamped in Etham, in the edge of the wilderness.

וַיהוָה הֹלֵךְ לִפְנֵיהֶם יוֹמָם בְּעַמּוּד עָנָן לַנְחֹתָם הַדֶּרֶךְ
the way   to lead them   cloud   in pillar   by day   before them   went   and ihvh

וְלַיְלָה בְּעַמּוּד אֵשׁ לְהָאִיר לָהֶם לָלֶכֶת יוֹמָם וָלָיְלָה׃
and night   by day   to go   to them   to the light   fire   in pillar   and night

21 And the LORD went before them by day in a pillar of a cloud, to lead them the way; and by night in a pillar of fire, to give them light; to go by day and night:

לֹא־יָמִישׁ עַמּוּד הֶעָנָן יוֹמָם וְעַמּוּד הָאֵשׁ לָיְלָה לִפְנֵי הָעָם׃
the people   before   night   the fire   and pillar   by day   the cloud   pillar   he remove - not

22 He took not away the pillar of the cloud by day, nor the pillar of fire by night, from before the people.

פ

Chapter 14

ספר שמות פרק יד

וַיְדַבֵּר יְהוָה אֶל־מֹשֶׁה לֵּאמֹר׃
to say   Moses – unto   ihvh   and he spoke

1 And the LORD spake unto Moses, saying,

דַּבֵּר אֶל־בְּנֵי יִשְׂרָאֵל וְיָשֻׁבוּ
and they return   Israel   sons – unto   speak

וְיַחֲנוּ לִפְנֵי פִּי הַחִירֹת בֵּין מִגְדֹּל וּבֵין הַיָּם
the sea   and between   Migdol   between   -- Pi-hahiroth --   before   and they tent

לִפְנֵי בַּעַל צְפֹן נִכְחוֹ תַחֲנוּ עַל־הַיָּם׃
the sea – upon   you tent   oposite   zephon   Baal   before

2 Speak unto the children of Israel, that they turn and encamp before Pi-hahiroth, between Migdol and the sea, over against Baal-zephon: before it shall ye encamp by the sea.

וְאָמַר פַּרְעֹה לִבְנֵי יִשְׂרָאֵל
Israel   to sons   Pharaoh   and said

נְבֻכִים הֵם בָּאָרֶץ סָגַר עֲלֵיהֶם הַמִּדְבָּר׃
the wilderness   upon them   closed   in land   them   entangled ones

3 For Pharaoh will say of the children of Israel, They are entangled in the land, the wilderness hath shut them in.

וְחִזַּקְתִּי אֶת־לֵב־פַּרְעֹה וְרָדַף אַחֲרֵיהֶם
after them   and will pursue   Pharaoh – heart – that   and I will harden

וְאִכָּבְדָ֤ה	בְּפַרְעֹה֙ וּבְכָל־חֵיל֔וֹ
and I will be honored	in Pharaoh his forces – and in all

וְיָדְע֥וּ	מִצְרַ֖יִם כִּֽי־אֲנִ֣י יְהוָ֑ה
and they will know	Egyptians I – like ihvh

וַיַּֽעֲשׂוּ־כֵֽן׃
thus – and they did

4 And I will harden Pharaoh's heart, that he shall follow after them; and I will be honoured upon Pharaoh, and upon all his host; that the Egyptians may know that I am the LORD. And they did so.

וַיֻּגַּד֙	לְמֶ֣לֶךְ מִצְרַ֔יִם כִּ֥י בָרַ֖ח הָעָ֑ם
and he told	to king Egyptian like fled the people

וַ֠יֵּהָפֵךְ	לְבַ֨ב פַּרְעֹ֤ה וַעֲבָדָיו֙ אֶל־הָעָ֔ם
and it changed	heart Pharaoh and his servants unto – the people

וַיֹּֽאמְרוּ֙	מַה־זֹּ֣את עָשִׂ֔ינוּ כִּֽי־שִׁלַּ֥חְנוּ אֶת־יִשְׂרָאֵ֖ל מֵעָבְדֵֽנוּ׃
and they said	what – this we did like – we sent that – Israel from serving us

5 And it was told the king of Egypt that the people fled: and the heart of Pharaoh and of his servants was turned against the people, and they said, Why have we done this, that we have let Israel go from serving us?

וַיֶּאְסֹ֖ר	אֶת־רִכְבּ֑וֹ וְאֶת־עַמּ֖וֹ לָקַ֥ח עִמּֽוֹ׃
and he hitched	his chariot – that his people – and that to take with him

6 And he made ready his chariot, and took his people with him:

וַיִּקַּ֗ח	שֵׁשׁ־מֵא֥וֹת רֶ֙כֶב֙ בָּח֔וּר
and he took hundred – six	chariots chosen

וְכֹ֖ל	רֶ֣כֶב מִצְרָ֑יִם וְשָׁלִשִׁ֖ם עַל־כֻּלּֽוֹ׃
and all	chariot Egyptian and captains upon – his all

7 And he took six hundred chosen chariots, and all the chariots of Egypt, and captains over every one of them.

וַיְחַזֵּ֣ק	יְהוָ֗ה אֶת־לֵ֤ב פַּרְעֹה֙ מֶ֣לֶךְ מִצְרַ֔יִם
and he hardened	ihvh heart – that Pharaoh King Egypt

וַיִּרְדֹּ֕ף	אַחֲרֵ֖י בְּנֵ֣י יִשְׂרָאֵ֑ל
and he pursued	after sons Israel

וּבְנֵ֣י	יִשְׂרָאֵ֔ל יֹצְאִ֖ים בְּיָ֥ד רָמָֽה׃
and sons	Israel going out ones in hand high place

8 And the LORD hardened the heart of Pharaoh king of Egypt, and he pursued after the children of Israel: and the children of Israel went out with an high hand.

[שני]

וַיִּרְדְּפוּ מִצְרַיִם אַחֲרֵיהֶם
and they pursued   Egyptians   after them

וַיַּשִּׂיגוּ אוֹתָם חֹנִים עַל־הַיָּם
and they overtook   to them   tenting ones   upon – the sea

כָּל־סוּס רֶכֶב פַּרְעֹה וּפָרָשָׁיו וְחֵילוֹ
all – horse   chariots   Pharaoh   and his horsemen   and his army

עַל־פִּי הַחִירֹת לִפְנֵי בַּעַל צְפֹן׃
Pi – upon   hahiroth   before   Baal   - zephon

9 But the Egyptians pursued after them, all the horses and chariots of Pharaoh, and his horsemen, and his army, and overtook them encamping by the sea, beside Pi-hahiroth, before Baal-zephon.

וּפַרְעֹה הִקְרִיב וַיִּשְׂאוּ בְנֵי־יִשְׂרָאֵל אֶת־עֵינֵיהֶם
and Pharaoh   drew near   and they lifted up   Israel – sons   that – their eyes

וְהִנֵּה מִצְרַיִם נֹסֵעַ אַחֲרֵיהֶם
and here   Egyptians   journeying   after them

וַיִּירְאוּ מְאֹד וַיִּצְעֲקוּ בְנֵי־יִשְׂרָאֵל אֶל־יְהוָה׃
and they afraid   greatly   and they cried out   Israel – sons   unto – ihvh

10 And when Pharaoh drew nigh, the children of Israel lifted up their eyes, and, behold, the Egyptians marched after them; and they were sore afraid: and the children of Israel cried out unto the LORD.

וַיֹּאמְרוּ אֶל־מֹשֶׁה
and they said   unto – Moses

הֲמִבְּלִי אֵין־קְבָרִים בְּמִצְרַיִם לְקַחְתָּנוּ לָמוּת בַּמִּדְבָּר
the from lack   isn't – graves   in Egypt   to take us   to die   in wilderness

מַה־זֹּאת עָשִׂיתָ לָּנוּ לְהוֹצִיאָנוּ מִמִּצְרָיִם׃
what – this   you did   to us   to take us out   from Egypt

11 And they said unto Moses, Because there were no graves in Egypt, hast thou taken us away to die in the wilderness? wherefore hast thou dealt thus with us, to carry us forth out of Egypt?

הֲלֹא־זֶה הַדָּבָר אֲשֶׁר דִּבַּרְנוּ אֵלֶיךָ בְמִצְרַיִם לֵאמֹר
not the – this   the matter   which   spoke us   unto you   in Egypt   to say

חֲדַל מִמֶּנּוּ וְנַעַבְדָה אֶת־מִצְרָיִם
leave off   from us   and we serve   that – Egyptians

כִּי טוֹב לָנוּ עֲבֹד אֶת־מִצְרַיִם מִמֻּתֵנוּ בַּמִּדְבָּר׃
like   good   to us   serving   that – Egyptians   dieing from us   in wilderness

102   PARASHAT 4   CHAPTER 14

12 Is not this the word that we did tell thee in Egypt, saying, Let us alone, that we may serve the Egyptians? For it had been better for us to serve the Egyptians, than that we should die in the wilderness.

וַיֹּאמֶר מֹשֶׁה אֶל־הָעָם אַל־תִּירָאוּ הִתְיַצְּבוּ
cause you to stand　fear you it – don't　the people – unto　Moses and he said

וּרְאוּ אֶת־יְשׁוּעַת יְהֹוָה אֲשֶׁר־יַעֲשֶׂה לָכֶם הַיּוֹם
the day　to you　he does – which　ihvh　salvation – that　and you see

כִּי אֲשֶׁר רְאִיתֶם אֶת־מִצְרַיִם הַיּוֹם
the day　Egyptians – that　you see　which　like

לֹא תֹסִפוּ לִרְאֹתָם עוֹד עַד־עוֹלָם׃
forever – till　again　to see them　you will continue　not

13 And Moses said unto the people, Fear ye not, stand still, and see the salvation of the LORD, which he will shew to you today: for the Egyptians whom ye have seen today, ye shall see them again no more for ever.

יְהֹוָה יִלָּחֵם לָכֶם וְאַתֶּם תַּחֲרִשׁוּן׃
you will be silent　and that you　to you　he fights　ihvh

14 The LORD shall fight for you, and ye shall hold your peace.

פ
[שלישי]

וַיֹּאמֶר יְהֹוָה אֶל־מֹשֶׁה מַה־תִּצְעַק אֵלָי
unto me　you cry – what　Moses – unto　ihvh　and he said

דַּבֵּר אֶל־בְּנֵי־יִשְׂרָאֵל וְיִסָּעוּ׃
and they journey　Israel – sons – unto　speak

15 And the LORD said unto Moses, Wherefore criest thou unto me? speak unto the children of Israel, that they go forward:

וְאַתָּה הָרֵם אֶת־מַטְּךָ וּנְטֵה אֶת־יָדְךָ עַל־הַיָּם
the sea – upon　your hand – that　and stretch out　your rod – that　the high　and you

וּבְקָעֵהוּ
and split it

וְיָבֹאוּ בְנֵי־יִשְׂרָאֵל בְּתוֹךְ הַיָּם בַּיַּבָּשָׁה׃
in dry land　the sea　in midst　Israel – sons　and they will come

16 But lift thou up thy rod, and stretch out thine hand over the sea, and divide it: and the children of Israel shall go on dry ground through the midst of the sea.

וַאֲנִי הִנְנִי מְחַזֵּק אֶת־לֵב מִצְרַיִם וְיָבֹאוּ אַחֲרֵיהֶם
after them　and they will come　Egyptians　heart – that　steadfast　here I　and I

PARASHAT 4　CHAPTER 14

וְאִכָּבְדָ֤ה בְּפַרְעֹה֙ וּבְכָל־חֵיל֔וֹ בְּרִכְבּ֖וֹ וּבְפָרָשָֽׁיו׃
and in his horsemen · in his chariots · his forces – and in all · in Pharaoh · and I will be honored

17 And I, behold, I will harden the hearts of the Egyptians, and they shall follow them: and I will get me honor upon Pharaoh, and upon all his host, upon his chariots, and upon his horsemen.

וְיָדְע֥וּ מִצְרַ֖יִם כִּֽי־אֲנִ֣י יְהֹוָ֑ה
ihvh · I – like · Egyptians · and they will know

בְּהִכָּבְדִ֥י בְּפַרְעֹ֖ה בְּרִכְבּ֥וֹ וּבְפָרָשָֽׁיו׃
and in his horsemen · in his chariots · in Pharaoh · in honoring me

18 And the Egyptians shall know that I am the LORD, when I have gotten me honour upon Pharaoh, upon his chariots, and upon his horsemen.

וַיִּסַּ֞ע מַלְאַ֣ךְ הָאֱלֹהִ֗ים הַהֹלֵךְ֙ לִפְנֵי֙ מַחֲנֵ֣ה יִשְׂרָאֵ֔ל
Israel · encampment · before · the walk · the Elohim · angel · and he journeyed

וַיֵּ֖לֶךְ מֵאַחֲרֵיהֶ֑ם וַיִּסַּ֞ע עַמּ֤וּד הֶֽעָנָן֙ מִפְּנֵיהֶ֔ם
from before them · the cloud · pillar · and it journeyed · from after them · and he went

וַיַּֽעֲמֹ֖ד מֵאַחֲרֵיהֶֽם׃
from after them · and it stood

19 And the angel of God, which went before the camp of Israel, removed and went behind them; and the pillar of the cloud went from before their face, and stood behind them:

וַיָּבֹ֞א בֵּ֣ין ׀ מַחֲנֵ֣ה מִצְרַ֗יִם וּבֵין֙ מַחֲנֵ֣ה יִשְׂרָאֵ֔ל
Israel · camp · and between · Egyptians · camp · between · and it came

וַיְהִ֤י הֶֽעָנָן֙ וְהַחֹ֔שֶׁךְ וַיָּ֖אֶר אֶת־הַלָּ֑יְלָה
the night – that · and it shined · and the darkness · the cloud · and it was

וְלֹא־קָרַ֥ב זֶ֛ה אֶל־זֶ֖ה כָּל־הַלָּֽיְלָה׃
the night – all · this – unto · this · neared – and not

20 And it came between the camp of the Egyptians and the camp of Israel; and it was a cloud and darkness to them, but it gave light by night to these: so that the one came not near the other all the night.

וַיֵּ֨ט מֹשֶׁ֣ה אֶת־יָדוֹ֮ עַל־הַיָּם֒
the sea – upon · his hand – that · Moses · and he stretched

וַיּ֣וֹלֶךְ יְהֹוָ֣ה ׀ אֶת־הַ֠יָּם בְּר֨וּחַ קָדִ֤ים עַזָּה֙ כָּל־הַלַּ֔יְלָה
in the night – all · strong · east · in wind · the sea – that · ihvh · and he went

וַיָּ֥שֶׂם אֶת־הַיָּ֖ם לֶחָרָבָ֑ה
to drain · the sea – that · and he put

וַיִּבָּקְע֖וּ הַמָּֽיִם׃
the sea · and they split

21 And Moses stretched out his hand over the sea; and the LORD caused the sea to go back by a strong east wind all that night, and made the sea dry land, and the waters were divided.

וַיָּבֹאוּ בְנֵי־יִשְׂרָאֵל בְּתוֹךְ הַיָּם בַּיַּבָּשָׁה
and they came   Israel – sons   in midst   the sea   in dry land

וְהַמַּיִם לָהֶם חוֹמָה מִימִינָם וּמִשְּׂמֹאלָם׃
and the sea   to them   wall   from their right   and from their left

22 And the children of Israel went into the midst of the sea upon the dry ground: and the waters were a wall unto them on their right hand, and on their left.

וַיִּרְדְּפוּ מִצְרַיִם וַיָּבֹאוּ אַחֲרֵיהֶם
and they pursued   Egyptians   and they came   after them

כֹּל סוּס פַּרְעֹה רִכְבּוֹ וּפָרָשָׁיו אֶל־תּוֹךְ הַיָּם׃
all   horse   Pharaoh   his chariot   and his horsemen   midst – unto   the sea

23 And the Egyptians pursued, and went in after them to the midst of the sea, even all Pharaoh's horses, his chariots, and his horsemen.

וַיְהִי בְּאַשְׁמֹרֶת הַבֹּקֶר
and it was   in vigil   the morning

וַיַּשְׁקֵף יְהוָה אֶל־מַחֲנֵה מִצְרַיִם בְּעַמּוּד אֵשׁ וְעָנָן
and he gazed   ihvh   camp – unto   Egyptians   in pillar   fire   and cloud

וַיָּהָם אֵת מַחֲנֵה מִצְרָיִם׃
and he troubled   that   camp   Egyptians

24 And it came to pass, that in the morning watch the LORD looked unto the host of the Egyptians through the pillar of fire and of the cloud, and troubled the host of the Egyptians,

וַיָּסַר אֵת אֹפַן מַרְכְּבֹתָיו וַיְנַהֲגֵהוּ בִּכְבֵדֻת
and he removed   that   wheel   from his chariot   and he drove it   in heavily

וַיֹּאמֶר מִצְרַיִם אָנוּסָה מִפְּנֵי יִשְׂרָאֵל
and he said   Egyptians   I flee   from face   Israel

כִּי יְהוָה נִלְחָם לָהֶם בְּמִצְרָיִם׃
like   ihvh   fights   to them   in Egyptians

25 And took off their chariot wheels, that they drave them heavily: so that the Egyptians said, Let us flee from the face of Israel; for the LORD fighteth for them against the Egyptians.

פ

[רביעי]

וַיֹּאמֶר יְהוָה אֶל־מֹשֶׁה נְטֵה אֶת־יָדְךָ עַל־הַיָּם
and he said ihvh Moses–unto stretch your hand–that the sea–upon

וְיָשֻׁבוּ הַמַּיִם עַל־מִצְרַיִם עַל־רִכְבּוֹ וְעַל־פָּרָשָׁיו׃
and they will return the waters upon–Egypt upon–his chariots and upon–his horsemen

26 And the LORD said unto Moses, Stretch out thine hand over the sea, that the waters may come again upon the Egyptians, upon their chariots, and upon their horsemen.

וַיֵּט מֹשֶׁה אֶת־יָדוֹ עַל־הַיָּם
and he stretched Moses that–his hand upon–the sea

וַיָּשָׁב הַיָּם לִפְנוֹת בֹּקֶר לְאֵיתָנוֹ
and it retuned the sea before morning to its constant flow

וּמִצְרַיִם נָסִים לִקְרָאתוֹ
and Egyptians fleeing ones to its meet

וַיְנַעֵר יְהוָה אֶת־מִצְרַיִם בְּתוֹךְ הַיָּם׃
and he shaked off ihvh that–Egyptians in midst the sea

27 And Moses stretched forth his hand over the sea, and the sea returned to his strength when the morning appeared; and the Egyptians fled against it; and the LORD overthrew the Egyptians in the midst of the sea.

וַיָּשֻׁבוּ הַמַּיִם
and they returned the waters

וַיְכַסּוּ אֶת־הָרֶכֶב וְאֶת־הַפָּרָשִׁים
and they covered that–the chariot and that–the horsemen

לְכֹל חֵיל פַּרְעֹה הַבָּאִים אַחֲרֵיהֶם בַּיָּם
to all force Pharaoh the coming ones after them in sea

לֹא־נִשְׁאַר בָּהֶם עַד־אֶחָד׃
not–remained in them till–one

28 And the waters returned, and covered the chariots, and the horsemen, and all the host of Pharaoh that came into the sea after them; there remained not so much as one of them.

וּבְנֵי יִשְׂרָאֵל הָלְכוּ בַיַּבָּשָׁה בְּתוֹךְ הַיָּם
and sons Israel they walked in dry land in midst the sea

וְהַמַּיִם לָהֶם חֹמָה מִימִינָם וּמִשְּׂמֹאלָם׃
and the water to them wall from their right and from their left

29 But the children of Israel walked upon dry land in the midst of the sea; and the waters were a wall unto them on their right hand, and on their left.

106 PARASHAT 4 CHAPTER 14

וַיּ֨וֹשַׁע יְהוָ֜ה בַּיּ֥וֹם הַה֛וּא אֶת־יִשְׂרָאֵ֖ל מִיַּ֣ד מִצְרָ֑יִם
 Egyptians from hand Israel – that the it in day ihvh and he saved

וַיַּ֤רְא יִשְׂרָאֵל֙ אֶת־מִצְרַ֔יִם מֵ֖ת עַל־שְׂפַ֥ת הַיָּֽם׃
 the sea shore – upon dead Egyptians – that Israel and he saw

30 Thus the LORD saved Israel that day out of the hand of the Egyptians; and Israel saw the Egyptians dead upon the sea shore.

וַיַּ֨רְא יִשְׂרָאֵ֜ל אֶת־הַיָּ֣ד הַגְּדֹלָ֗ה אֲשֶׁ֨ר עָשָׂ֤ה יְהוָה֙ בְּמִצְרַ֔יִם
 in Egypt ihvh did which the great the hand – that Israel and he saw

וַיִּֽירְא֥וּ הָעָ֖ם אֶת־יְהוָ֑ה
 ihvh – that the people and they feared

וַיַּֽאֲמִ֨ינוּ֙ בַּֽיהוָ֔ה וּבְמֹשֶׁ֖ה עַבְדּֽוֹ׃
 his servant and in Moses in ihvh and they believed

31 And Israel saw that great work which the LORD did upon the Egyptians: and the people feared the LORD, and believed the LORD, and his servant Moses.

                   פ

Chapter 15

ספר שמות פרק טו

אָ֣ז יָשִֽׁיר־מֹשֶׁה֩ וּבְנֵ֨י יִשְׂרָאֵ֜ל
 Israel and sons Moses – he sang then

אֶת־הַשִּׁירָ֤ה הַזֹּאת֙
 the this the song – that

לַֽיהוָ֔ה וַיֹּאמְר֖וּ לֵאמֹ֑ר
 to ihvh and they said to say

אָשִׁ֤ירָה לַֽיהוָה֙ כִּֽי־גָאֹ֣ה גָּאָ֔ה ס֥וּס וְרֹכְב֖וֹ רָמָ֥ה בַיָּֽם׃
 in sea to high and his rider horse gloriously glorious – like to ihvh I sing

1 Then sang Moses and the children of Israel this song unto the LORD, and spake, saying, I will sing unto the LORD, for he hath triumphed gloriously: the horse and his rider hath he thrown into the sea.

עָזִּ֤י וְזִמְרָת֙ יָ֔הּ וַֽיְהִי־לִ֖י לִֽישׁוּעָ֑ה
 to salvation to me – and is Ya and melody my strength

זֶ֤ה אֵלִי֙ וְאַנְוֵ֔הוּ אֱלֹהֵ֥י אָבִ֖י וַאֲרֹמְמֶֽנְהוּ׃
 and I will exalt him my father Elohim and I adorn him my El that

2 The LORD is my strength and song, and he is become my salvation: he is my God, and I will prepare him an habitation; my father's God, and I will exalt him.

יְהוָה אִישׁ מִלְחָמָה יְהוָה שְׁמוֹ:
his name   ihvh   war   man   ihvh

3 The LORD is a man of war: the LORD is his name.

מַרְכְּבֹת פַּרְעֹה וְחֵילוֹ יָרָה בַיָּם
in sea   he shot   and his force   Pharaoh   from chariots

וּמִבְחַר שָׁלִשָׁיו טֻבְּעוּ בְיַם־סוּף:
end - in sea   they sank   his captains   and chosen

4 Pharaoh's chariots and his host hath he cast into the sea: his chosen captains also are drowned in the Red sea.

תְּהֹמֹת יְכַסְיֻמוּ יָרְדוּ בִמְצוֹלֹת כְּמוֹ־אָבֶן:
stone – like   in dark depths   they descended   they covered him   depths

5 The depths have covered them: they sank into the bottom as a stone.

יְמִינְךָ יְהוָה נֶאְדָּרִי בַּכֹּחַ
in power   ennobled   ihvh   your right hand

יְמִינְךָ יְהוָה תִּרְעַץ אוֹיֵב:
enemy   break in pieces   ihvh   your right hand

6 Thy right hand, O LORD, is become glorious in power: thy right hand, O LORD, hath dashed in pieces the enemy.

וּבְרֹב גְּאוֹנְךָ תַּהֲרֹס קָמֶיךָ
your arisers   demolishing   your pomp   and in much

תְּשַׁלַּח חֲרֹנְךָ יֹאכְלֵמוֹ כַּקַּשׁ:
stubble   he consumed them   your fury   you sent forth

7 And in the greatness of thine excellency thou hast overthrown them that rose up against thee: thou sentest forth thy wrath, which consumed them as stubble.

וּבְרוּחַ אַפֶּיךָ נֶעֶרְמוּ מַיִם
water   they gathered together   your nose   and in wind

נִצְּבוּ כְמוֹ־נֵד נֹזְלִים קָפְאוּ תְהֹמֹת בְּלֶב־יָם:
sea - in heart   depths   they settled   floods   waterspout - like   they stood upright

8 And with the blast of thy nostrils the waters were gathered together, the floods stood upright as an heap, and the depths were congealed in the heart of the sea.

אָמַר אוֹיֵב אֶרְדֹּף אַשִּׂיג אֲחַלֵּק שָׁלָל
plunder   I will apportion   I will overtake   I will pursue   enemy   said

תִּמְלָאֵמוֹ נַפְשִׁי אָרִיק חַרְבִּי תּוֹרִישֵׁמוֹ יָדִי:
my hand   it will evict them   my sword   I will unsheathe   my soul   it fulfilled them

9 The enemy said, I will pursue, I will overtake, I will divide the spoil; my lust

shall be satisfied upon them; I will draw my sword, my hand shall destroy them.

נָשַׁפְתָּ בְרוּחֲךָ כִּסָּמוֹ יָם
you blew　in your wind　covered them　sea

צָלֲלוּ כַּעוֹפֶרֶת בְּמַיִם אַדִּירִים׃
they submerged　like lead　in waters　mighty ones

10 Thou didst blow with thy wind, the sea covered them: they sank as lead in the mighty waters.

מִי־כָמֹכָה בָּאֵלִם יְהֹוָה
ihvh　in Elohim　like you - who

מִי כָּמֹכָה נֶאְדָּר בַּקֹּדֶשׁ
who　like you　being nobel　in holiness

נוֹרָא תְהִלֹּת עֹשֵׂה פֶלֶא׃
fearful　praises　doing　wonders

11 Who is like unto thee, O LORD, among the gods? who is like thee, glorious in holiness, fearful in praises, doing wonders?

נָטִיתָ יְמִינְךָ תִּבְלָעֵמוֹ אָרֶץ׃
you stretched　your right hand　it swallowed them　earth

12 Thou stretchedst out thy right hand, the earth swallowed them.

נָחִיתָ בְחַסְדְּךָ עַם־זוּ גָּאָלְתָּ
you led　in your mercy　that - people　you redeemed

נֵהַלְתָּ בְעָזְּךָ אֶל־נְוֵה קָדְשֶׁךָ׃
you conduct　in your strength　habitation - unto　your holy

13 Thou in thy mercy hast led forth the people which thou hast redeemed: thou hast guided them in thy strength unto thy holy habitation.

שָׁמְעוּ עַמִּים יִרְגָּזוּן חִיל אָחַז יֹשְׁבֵי פְּלָשֶׁת׃
they will hear　people　will be disturbed　travail　takes hold　dwellers　Philistia

14 The people shall hear, and be afraid: sorrow shall take hold on the inhabitants of Palestina.

אָז נִבְהֲלוּ אַלּוּפֵי אֱדוֹם
thence　they flustered　chiefs　Edom

אֵילֵי מוֹאָב יֹאחֲזֵמוֹ רָעַד
arbiters　Moab　will take hold them　trembling

נָמֹגוּ כֹּל יֹשְׁבֵי כְנָעַן׃
they dissolved　all　dwellers　Canaan

15 Then the dukes of Edom shall be amazed; the mighty men of Moab, trembling shall take hold upon them; all the inhabitants of Canaan shall melt away.

תִּפֹּל	עֲלֵיהֶם	אֵימָתָה	וָפַחַד
you fall	upon them	dread	and awe

בִּגְדֹל	זְרוֹעֲךָ	יִדְּמוּ	כָּאָבֶן
in great	your arm	they still	like stone

עַד־יַעֲבֹר	עַמְּךָ	יְהוָה
passover – till	your people	ihvh

עַד־יַעֲבֹר	עַם־זוּ	קָנִיתָ׃
passover - till	that - people	you purchased

16 Fear and dread shall fall upon them; by the greatness of thine arm they shall be as still as a stone; till thy people pass over, O LORD, till the people pass over, which thou hast purchased.

תְּבִאֵמוֹ	וְתִטָּעֵמוֹ	בְּהַר	נַחֲלָתְךָ
you will bring them	and you plant them	in mountain	your inheritance

מָכוֹן	לְשִׁבְתְּךָ	פָּעַלְתָּ	יְהוָה
place	to your dwelling	you acted	ihvh

מִקְּדָשׁ	אֲדֹנָי	כּוֹנְנוּ	יָדֶיךָ׃
sanctuary	Adoni	established	your hand

17 Thou shalt bring them in, and plant them in the mountain of thine inheritance, in the place, O LORD, which thou hast made for thee to dwell in, in the Sanctuary, O Lord, which thy hands have established.

יְהוָה	יִמְלֹךְ	לְעֹלָם	וָעֶד׃
ihvh	he will reign	forever	and ever

18 The LORD shall reign for ever and ever.

כִּי	בָא	סוּס	פַּרְעֹה	בְּרִכְבּוֹ	וּבְפָרָשָׁיו	בַּיָּם
like	came	horse	Pharaoh	in his chariot	and in his horsemen	in sea

וַיָּשֶׁב	יְהוָה	עֲלֵהֶם	אֶת־מֵי	הַיָּם
and he returned	ihvh	upon them	water – that	the sea

וּבְנֵי	יִשְׂרָאֵל	הָלְכוּ	בַיַּבָּשָׁה	בְּתוֹךְ	הַיָּם׃
and sons	Israel	they went	in dry land	in midst	the sea

19 For the horse of Pharaoh went in with his chariots and with his horsemen into the sea, and the LORD brought again the waters of the sea upon them; but the children of Israel went on dry land in the midst of the sea.

www.ingramcontent.com/pod-product-compliance
Lightning Source LLC
Chambersburg PA
CBHW070522030426
42337CB00016B/2065